William Renton

The logic of style

being an introduction to critical science

William Renton

The logic of style
being an introduction to critical science

ISBN/EAN: 9783742815743

Manufactured in Europe, USA, Canada, Australia, Japa

Cover: Foto ©Thomas Meinert / pixelio.de

Manufactured and distributed by brebook publishing software
(www.brebook.com)

William Renton

The logic of style

THE
LOGIC OF STYLE

BEING

AN INTRODUCTION TO

Critical Science

By WILLIAM RENTON

LONDON
LONGMANS, GREEN, & CO.
1874

CONTENTS.

—— ——...

	PAGE
INTRODUCTION BY WAY OF PREFACE, . . .	1

CHAPTER I.

OF STYLE GENERALLY.

Section I. Of Expression Generally, §§ 1—3, . . .	41
Section II. Of Style in its relation to Expression, §§ 4—6, .	54
Section III. Of Style in its relation to Rhetoric, §§ 7—9, . . .	60

CHAPTER II.

OF QUALITY.

Section I. The Conditions of Quality, §§ 10—12, . . .	80
Section II. Of Subtlety, §§ 13—15, . . .	89
Section III. Of Comprehensiveness, §§ 16—18, . .	103

CHAPTER III.

OF QUANTITY.

Section I. The Principle of Quantity, §§ 19.—21, . .	121
Section II. Of Extension (Co-ordination), §§ 22—24, . .	130
Section III. Of Intension (Subordination), §§ 25—27, . .	139

INTRODUCTION

BY WAY OF PREFACE.

——•——

It is a cumbrous disadvantage for an Introduction to a Theory of Style, that Style, as a science, stands so closely in interconnection with other sciences. This connection, on the one hand, is one of coincidence, on the other, of analogy. In the one instance, the science seems to support itself on the facts of the correlative sciences, in the other, on their principles. And so it is forced into relations that are too obvious to be repudiated, even while they are too numerous not to interfere with its free expansion as an independent system.

This disadvantage, the most awkward that can arise for any theory claiming for its phenomena a distinct genesis and a distinct economy, is at the same time one of the least obvious. Not that the multiplicity in the relationships of Style to other subjects has been overlooked; since it is the too common experience that mere redundancy of suggestion tends often to confound and perplex. Besides, from the opposite point of view, it could not fail to be noted, that, in the midst of any such redundancy, a certain proportion of ease must have attended the work of recombining materials which other sciences had discovered, or of organizing fresh

materials according to rules which they had suggested. The
difficulty of the case is hidden by a prior misunderstanding
as to the true scope of Style. And it arises from the doubt
as to whether Style is to be regarded as a science at all,
and as such in a position to be illuminated—with the privilege of reciprocal illumination—by any science whatsoever.

To the ordinary way of thinking, nothing more is required
for a science than that the facts which it provides shall be
susceptible of a logical classification. But there is also the
negative condition of qualification—viz., that the science shall
have its own lawful complement of facts. In the present
case, Style is regarded somehow as a galaxy of miscellaneous
truths, chiefly of truths practical and applied. If as a science
it is to be considered, it seems to withdraw itself into such
a science as Logic; so that ultimately it *is* no science, wanting an independent basis. But in this there is the natural
oversight, that certain facts, however eagerly they may sub-
mit to the rules of a system like Logic, as a primary source
of administration, may yet be susceptible of a *secondary* treatment and valuation. Practical Style may be; yet, examined
philosophically, it will be found to include a nucleus of
theoretic principles, to which, more immediately than to those
of Logic, its facts may be referred. This skeleton of principle
it is, this nucleus—whether it be one according to which
certain facts common to all mental science are treated, or a
derivative order of facts, or facts entirely original—which
constitutes the Science of Style.

For the coherent exposition of its own facts a theory
requires a tolerably large compass. But, within that compass,
and in the particular illustration of its facts, a science will
infallibly ratify its claim to having special data. The more

unique its position theoretically, the more striking its interpretation of these data. But the burden of doing explicitly and by anticipation what the science itself does implicitly, descends upon the Introduction, which has to show with precision what the principle is, according to which phenomena that apparently have been pre-engrossed by sciences more lucky or more precocious, may be treated, virtually, or in fact, as new. The negative condition being thus satisfied, Style vaults airily into the cycle of the sciences. But this ennobling of Style, in claiming a scientific lineage for a certain order of facts, involves the enlarging of the conception of science itself. Hence, in the second place, it devolves upon an Introduction to Style to reflect a principle upon science generally, as discovering a new variety of adaptation, and possibly of treatment. Bringing thus for the principle of science fresh facts, it brings for the facts of science a fresh principle. And so its two aims or results coincide. For the principle, under which the facts have been discovered to be amenable to scientific analysis, is precisely the principle which must underlie and coincide with the supplementary extension given to the notion of science. An incidental result is that the scientific meaning of certain acknowledged facts is established, where it was believed to be impossible; and a profounder and more emphatic, because more precise and consistent, recognition given of them in regions, where, if in part formally recognised, they were virtually, and in their distinctive principle, denied.

An operative, and, practically, a new distinction is introduced into science, when a division is made of the Subjective or Mental sciences into those which are concerned with Sensibility, and those which are not. The facts, and through the facts, the laws of Style, and, in a greater degree, of Music, are not to be obtained at first hand by every one. They are to be gathered only through a special medium, superadded to the intellectual medium which is essential to all scientific exposition. To Logic, however, as a branch of mental science, the term Subjective does not apply in the philosophic sense. Its phenomena are severely objective, in so far as they may be observed by everybody, and yield principles which each one may test for himself. In the same way, the facts of Style, though subject to a greater fluctuation and diversity than those of Logic, are also objective, in the sense that ulti- mately they rest on a common sensibility, not necessarily morbid in cases where it is high, nor coarse where it is low. The variations of individual, *i.e.* truly subjective, sensibility are infinite. But it is on that account precisely that a wary science will refuse to compromise itself by an explana- tion of facts, that, *ex hypothesi*, are too numerous to be explained. Such an explanation would be impossible. It would also be suicidal. For it is only with these variations as recurrent, and having essential points of agreement, and a catholic significance, that the science is concerned. All beyond that is isolated, in many cases contradictory. And with individual bias or eccentricity, even in a god, science has nothing to do. The limit, therefore, at which Style ceases to be objective, is where it ceases to transcend indi- vidual peculiarity, and where effects become local and capri- cious. At the same time, and while ultimately there is no difference in this respect, a distinction may be made between Style and Logic on the ground of the greater evasiveness of its phenomena, because adding an element distinct from that which makes the logical phenomena themselves evasive as distinct from those of Physical Science. The sciences fall most conveniently, therefore, into this order, the Physical, the Philosophical, and the Æsthetic or Critical. The distinction is valid for ordinary purposes, and must be insisted on for Style, especially in its relation to Logic, as occupying a station intermediate between it and the Natural Sciences—which relation is now illustrated in detail.

1. Style, together with Logic, may in part be distinguished from the Physical Sciences by the less palpable nature of its phenomena, and, contingently, by the greater precariousness of its method. But it is also to be distinguished by the fact of being more stationary as a system. Not that mental science, as, for example, in the form of Psychology, where discoveries are constantly being registered, is not progressive as a whole, but, in certain fields belonging more exclusively to speculative analysis, it *is* improgressive. And a test (which must be verified historically) may thus be applied to discriminate the pure sections in philosophy from the mixed or derivative. Accordingly, those which at the very first are capable of a complete integration, go into the category of the cardinal sciences, and those which are not, into that of the derivative sciences. The facts of Style, in contradistinction to those of Physical Science, may be collected in virtual completeness by one single observer. The theory is not one that depends on a complementary observation extending over an indefinite period of time. And so Style ranges itself, along with Logic and Grammar, under the category of Pure Mental Science.

Notwithstanding this, there is no privileged road to discovery in Logic or in Style, other than that of severe

observation and reflection, by which science universally
travels, so haughtily as regards its warrant, so patiently
as regards its results. It is precisely as evanescent, and
requiring a keener observation, that their phenomena are
discarded for others of a more palpable character. Certainly
there is no monopoly created for Style by the mere opportunities which the individual theorist has for inquiry.
Scientific success does not go according to the *mechanical*
facilities which one man has, as compared with another, for
collecting facts—is not given gratuitously—but goes according to individual capacity for the collation of facts, for
observation and generalization. Else the savage has more
opportunity of naturalistic acquirement, because more of
naturalistic research, than the man of culture. Hence
it is that mere perception of effects is not operative in
all men alike, nor mediately to the same results. In Style,
for example, the power to write idiomatically and with precision does not confer the power of scientific analysis; the
two in all likelihood exist inversely as each other. But the
literary power may evidently become a desirable co-efficient
in an analysis that is dedicated exclusively to literary phenomena. And, in an analysis which aims at a precision as
perfect as that attainable under any other science, it is too
evidently an indispensable co-efficient. Hence the main distinction between Logic and Style, in a sensibility which
supplies the facts that are to be logically explained; having,
in so far, no value for Logic, but, on the other hand, being
invaluable for Æsthetic Criticism.

2. Sensibility is, accordingly, the element which distinguishes a logical from an æsthetic science. Not, however,
in the sense of being antagonistic to logical analysis. On the

contrary, it is of no value in science without that. For literary science, therefore, considered in its unity, each is reciprocally indispensable to the other. The same truth is expressed in saying that Sensibility is the negative condition for all systematic inquiry in the region of literary effect; as may be illustrated historically in relation to Style itself.

Strictly speaking, Style has no history. For a history demands a unity of subject, with a series of developments more or less marked and continuous. The only interest that Style can have is, in this view, a negative and exoteric interest. Considered under this limitation, therefore, Style resolves itself historically into two momenta, or crises, of which the appearance of Aristotle forms the first. It might seem curious, that, of two subjects lying parallel to each other, that one should be chosen for the richer and more explicit treatment, whose phenomena are, on the whole, the more recondite. A man is naturally more struck by the use of a barbarism in speech—i.e. it is more of an event for him, whether he mentions it to his wife or not—than by the fact that his neighbour is reasoning in a circle. But the grossest phenomena are not always the most suggestive. Especially are they not likely to be suggestive when they appeal to a capacity, which, not being exceptionally sensitive itself, is flanked by a capacity that *is* exceptional for perceiving and pursuing some other order of phenomena.

This is sufficient to explain, for the moment, why Logic rather than Literary Science should have met with a conclusive treatment at the hands of Aristotle. An attempt, it is true, was formally made by him to systematize the other class of facts. But it is clear that he did not apprehend the subject in its philosophic relations; else he would have seen that it is

precisely analogous to Logic—persistently and selfishly so—
complementary to it, and erecting itself beside it to whatever
extent, and in what direction soever it may be impelled.
Hence the subordinate place assigned to Style in his complete
system, as a suckling of Oratorical Science; and in such a
way as to thwart and vitiate its literary significance. Hence
also this very striking circumstance, connected with the fact
of its depreciation. Considered independently, Style allows
of an abstract treatment, in at least as great a degree as Logic.
Sensibility apart, the pure intellect may construct a speculative science of the subject for itself. How much more then
with the light reflected upon it so unequivocally by the
revelations of Logic. But, as in passing from one subject to
another, the two may be affected favourably by their intense
juxtaposition, so sometimes they may be mischievously
affected, and clash with each other. Having the first, a man
will the more readily have the second; or else, having the
first, he will *not* have the second. Either his conception of
the one, by implying the conception of the possible whole,
will suggest and illuminate the other; or else, by palming
itself off as the actual whole, will obscure the conception of
the other. This is, to a certain extent, the explanation of
the unimpartial treatment, so to speak, accorded to the
Rhetoric, as compared with the Organon, where, upon a
superficial view, brilliance of analysis might seem to have
been most required. Since if—and *if*, then precisely *because*,
his sensibility was not exceptional, Aristotle was bound to
supplement it by that which he had in abundance. The case,
however, was otherwise; theorizing, in the absence of sensibility, being simply impossible. But in part also the want
of susceptibility in this direction, which determined him to-

wards Logic, as a science promising a more unique and
opulent result, would determine him at the same time away
from Style, as a field that did not present phenomena con-
genial for exposition, and that did not, therefore, for *his*
subtlety furnish an adequate stage of illustration.

A proof of this appears in connection with the effects
which more particularly he *did* note. It was open to him to
have overlooked the whole body of literary appearances.
What he did overlook was that section which is least prominent and most characteristic. Limiting his view thus, he
concentrates attention upon those facts which it belongs to
the average sensibility to descry for itself, and which require
a very moderate effort to systematize. In this latter respect
it is that the Rhetoric of Aristotle compares so meagrely with
his Organon, and precisely because lacking, in its separate
sphere, a corresponding depth of perception. The section of
effects which the Rhetoric represents is concerned with that
identical sphere of perception which is the most common,
and, similarly, the Rhetoric itself is concerned with that
systematizing of effects, whose activity unfolds itself most
easily. Another sphere, which has been already indicated, is
that of the abstract science, in which the principles of Logic
and Style unfold concurrently. But the whole cycle of Stylic
science is not complete, until a third section of still more
complex effects is reduced to system. This order of effects is
more subtle and intricate than any with which the analyst
occupies himself in Logic. The dissertationist on Style in its
more abstract relations does not necessarily possess a command over this ultimate section; though he cannot investigate
it thoroughly without that command. But, having the qualifying sensibility, he will inevitably, in his analysis of it, recur

to the abstract science as his ultimate ground of reference. It is not to be wondered at, therefore, that, for want of this qualification, Aristotle should not have busied himself seriously with either the one section or the other—the accident of the Organon apart, as a possible cause predisposing to, or away from, an equally rigorous and determinative treatment of Style. Within a certain compass his own style is unexceptionably good. But of any extrinsic brilliance in his writing, or even of the art of manœuvring to advantage within the limits prescribed by philosophic exigencies, there is no trace. And, which is more important, to compensate for this want, there is no sign of any æsthetic perception of effects beyond those reproduced in his own practice. His critical susceptibility was not pitched (as it might quite well have been) upon a higher key than that to which he himself daily conformed. So that, as far as any acquaintance with the higher effects was concerned, it must have been drawn from the practice of his own countrymen. The Greeks, as a rule, compare favourably with other nations in this respect. As general practitioners in the art, they are always to be commended for imitation; and they excel in certain of the more essential qualities that go towards realizing a noble standard of composition. But that conspicuous excellence is wanting that might have suggested to a contemporary a very high, and, in connection with striking deformities of expression (which in this case were also wanting), a very practical and thoroughgoing, literary ideal.

So far, indeed, as Greece is concerned, critical science in Aristotle is not so far behind models of real excellence, as it is in the rear of such transcendent models as have appeared in England. The effect of such models, in stimulating

criticism and enlarging its area, will be determined by the
way in which these models unite to form a catholic ideal.
Even this chance, however, of accomplishing such an end
will be defeated, should the critic happen to be out of harmony with the scope of his materials, and busy himself with
the exposition of certain orders of excellence to the exclusion
of the rest. The greater, therefore, is the necessity for a
catholic sympathy that shall confirm, and not subvert, the
data, which, in having brought near to them the requisite
qualifications for their practical study are, *pro tanto*, brought
nearer to an appreciable result—a sympathy that shall not
falsify its claims in the moment of substantiating them. One
only case there is, in which this sympathy with pre-existing
effects may be dispensed with, that, viz., in which it is superseded by the accident of a critic who exhibits the principle
of these effects in himself. De Quincey, with unparalleled
compass of sensibility, and with great analytic acuteness,
might naturally have been expected to furnish a result in
which the two might effectively be combined. To the
materials that Aristotle lacked, he added the power that
was to ratify them; and, to such an extent, as not merely to
supersede the illustrations of older writers, if by chance they
had been orbicular enough in their sweep for an analysis to
found upon, but to anticipate the latest phases of creative
sensibility, if by chance these should not have been already
developed.

The appearance of De Quincey, in fact, constitutes the
second momentum in the history of Style. That this momentum is again a crisis, not an epoch, is due to the fact that the
possible advantages from a susceptibility so complex were
neutralized, for purposes of an exposition that should, in any

sense, be final, by his defect of energy for pure speculation.[1]
So much, at least, of negative constructiveness the world was
justified in expecting, as would have shattered the confusions
besieging the subject.   These to have exposed would seem to
have been suited to his peculiar ability and his peculiar *mettle*.
And that with a result the more favourable, as one might
have presumed, for the diffusion of critical knowledge, from
his rare power of philosophical exposition.   No difficulty that
he was not qualified to divest of any preternatural appearance of complexity or abstruseness: no problem whose
spurious simplicity he was not able to detect, and in its mis-
chievousness to counteract, by exposing it in that light which
was best calculated to reveal the lurking perplexity.   But
never was there a mind more fitted to mediate between philosophy and the popular good-will, that was more irretrievably
cut off from such communication, by a want of sympathy
with philosophy itself, precisely in those latitudes where a
facile exposition was most needed for the populace, because in
the general case most difficult to obtain from expositors, and
most demanded, because in his individual case most easy to
give.

   To this want so clamorous, to this crisis so bewitching, De
Quincey brought nothing but a gleam or two of critical
insight, and with a result that is naturally more tantalizing
than the shortcoming of Aristotle.   Against any such shortcoming, as detrimental to his general reputation, Aristotle
had virtually pleaded in the blazing originality of the Organon.

---

[1] This refers not to anything De Quincey failed to do, but evidently to some
positive misunderstanding of certain philosophic problems.   The reader of De
Quincey surmises that the special victim of this obliquity—but with no desire
on the part of the critic save to state the matter truthfully, and disarmed as
to the special misinterpretation by its very naïveté—was Kant.

And, which made the matter still more interesting, his power
in the Organon shone not merely by itself, but by an *involution* of itself, which upon the arena of Style might have
been illustrated, in a way more comprehensive and theatrical,
by De Quincey. What Aristotle effected had this peculiar
property, that it was effected by a movement of circularity.
It was the judgment itself occupied upon the judgment; and
such a judgment, occupied on such materials, as to produce a
result in which all men should virtually agree. Deny the
perfection of the judgment, and, *à priori*, you impugn the
truth of the system. Deny the truth of the system, and, *à
posteriori*, you infer the weakness of the judgment. Accepting
absolutely the thesis of Aristotle, you admit it as a criterion
of the process by which you pronounce upon the logic of the
thesis itself. Refusing to accept the thesis as true, you
imply, and are bound to produce, another explanation of that
very process by which you have discovered that the process
is other than that laid down by the theorist. By a parallel
chance in Style, a writer like De Quincey is practically the
exponent of the very principles which in theory he enunciates
and commends. Now, in such a case, it is the Sensibility
which forms the machinery of the involution. Lustre will
unquestionably be given to logical science by beauty of Style.
But this element is adventitious. It is not implicit in the
conception of Logic, as perceptive sympathy *is* implicit in the
conception of sensibility on such a scale as De Quincey's.
But Style, besides this element of sensibility, as inseparably
a condition for scientific exposition, demands also the more
palpable element of speculative insight. Where a science of
Logic demands one element, therefore, an adequate science of
Style demands two. And while Logic is thus its own expo-

nent, Style may be more illustriously so, because having an
involution of scientific insight the same in degree as that
of Logic, to which Logic, on its part, has nothing to answer
in the way of sensibility. This sensibility was neutralized
in De Quincey for its scientific application (despite his fas-
tidious thinking), by the want of that element, which, in the
converse case of Aristotle, was neutralized by the want of
the antithetic sensibility.

The antithesis, which is thus illustrated, is equally true in
relation to its two elements, whether existing in insulation
from each other, or aiding one another in a scientific rationale
of the whole field under review. What is easy to perceive is
pro tanto easy to systematize. And what tends, by its very
nature, to incarnate itself under universal distinctions is *pro
tanto* easy to perceive. And here, as suggesting itself from
the special contrast already indicated in the historical relations of both sciences, a general contrast may be drawn
between Style and Logic. Logic, in the Organon of Aristotle,
was then first recognised as a fact, when it was first recognised as a science. Its phenomena were first matter of general
observation, when their connecting principles were first
formally arranged in their relation to its dominant principle.
Style, on the other hand, has been long recognised as a fact—
certain even of its distinctions are current and popular—but
not earnestly and conscientiously as a science. And so long
as its main distinctions remain neither explicated, nor shown
in their propulsion, nor in their analogical relations, nor in
their speculative significance, there is nothing to contribute to
the science, much less the history, of the subject, which is
also the history of the science.

The final lesson, therefore, of the antithesis between the

two elements is that of their being mutually necessary to each
other, and, as it were, in a certain order; and precisely, for the
science, in *this* order, that it must presuppose and follow the
sensibility. Nothing, indeed, can be more self-evident than
that a man should be unable to give the rationale of certain
facts, when he does not perceive them, or does not perceive
them to the extent that they ought to be perceived. How,
for instance, should he expect to be listened to as a critic,
who pronounces a certain image to be sublime, or the cadence
of a certain passage to be harmonious, having no æsthetic
perception whatsoever? For in Style generally there may be
discriminated three classes of effects: (1) those which the
investigator sees in common with all, (2) those which he sees
in common with a few, and (3) those which possibly he sees
to the exclusion of everybody else. In view of this, and
relying upon the common ground of agreement which he has
with all, it is his business gradually to extend the frontier of
perception as far as he can—initiate the first class of readers
into the secrets of the second, and the second into those of the
third, along with such of the first class as have surmounted
the difficulties of the second sphere. Unless, indeed, he has
either something special to communicate, or some more concise or more fascinating method of communicating to the
many what as yet is only enjoyed by the few, or of impress-
ing upon all, from his station of authority, what is only held
vaguely, there is no justification for the obtrusion of his views.
But only as founding ultimately on a catholic sensibility, is
he warranted in putting the matter in such a way as to secure
interest for it, and attention for himself. Nor is this a
method which belongs to these facts as an insulated class of
facts. It is the method of the Fine Arts generally. In

Painting, for instance, besides the abstract science, which
treats of the general divisions of form and colour, &c., there
is the concrete science, which tells, according to the criterion
of the sensibility, why certain individual effects are beautiful,
or the opposite. Among such effects, it is the province of the
most ordinary sensibility to recognise the agreeable impression produced by clusters of scarlet berries upon a background
of green. But a subtler question arises, why it is that such
berries are more effective as seen on a tree with feathery
branches, than they would be on a yew tree, for example.
The reason generally is this :—The combination cannot fail to
benefit in effect by the greater disclosure of the wood of the
branches, as in the former case, and of the berries themselves;
leaves, berries, and branches forming, first, a perceptible
variety in material, next, one of colour, and, finally, a
graduated series in regard to stability (as under the possible
movements of the wind), which would not be available to the
same extent in the case of the obscuring branches of the yew.
But, specially, the difference is due (1) to the contrast of the
perky or pensile character of the leaves, in the former case,
with the solid and pendulous character of the berries—contrast, the sense of which would be stifled in regard to the
clotted or matted branches of the yew. And (2) in the case
of the tree which allows for so much variegation in the superficial outline, and, as it were, so much general transparency,
there is a chance of both leaves and berries being relieved
against a *common* background.

3. In thus discovering itself to be a Fine Art, Style is not
to be distinguished from Logic, as if it were something
superior, merely because it has something superadded. Any
superiority which it can show must rest upon its value,

considered teleologically. Here, nevertheless, a practical
superiority is claimed for Style. Not that its aim is absolutely higher than the aim of any art which proposes to
redress the inequalities, and correct the infirmities, of the
human judgment. No intellectual aim can possibly be so
high. Besides, the improvement of the catholic judgment, in
so far as it is corrigible by rules, involves an education
generally for other purposes, by which Art itself must ultimately profit. But the lower art as to aim may yet happen
to approximate more closely to its aim than the higher. The
defence, therefore, which might apply to Logic, as a science
that must be examined formally, before it can yield its full
quota of practical results (notwithstanding that these results
are concerned with rules whose application must already be
presupposed), is irrelevant to Style. For while in Logic the
alternatives are few, under which effects are good or bad, the
particularization of which Style is capable admits of an
indefinite number of examples of good or of vicious expression
being given, having all the vividness of a circumstantial
treatment and all the force of a general principle. It thus
provides for a graduated improvement, to which Logic (as
universally understood) makes no pretension. The reason of
this is plain. In so far as Style is complex, it allows of a
specific treatment in a degree unattainable by Logic;—for the
same reason a history of Universal Literature is evidently a
much subtler problem than a history of Philosophy. But by
Logic in what guise is this unattainable? It is as being
formally too simple. A certain fallacy may be seen, and not
only seen, but seen to come under a special principle and
category of fallacy; and yet the man who sees it may be
unable to bring it home to the man who uses it, and who per-

sists that his argument does not come within that category.
Did Logic seek to go beyond this, its boundaries would be
inordinately enlarged, and it would have to descend to impossible details. The objection to it in such a case would be, not
that it is too simple, but that it is too complex. And if the
logician will descend into the region of material truth, he
must not be disgusted to find that his researches are circum-
scribed and arbitrary. It is significant, therefore, in this
connection, when such a man chooses his illustrations from
science: when he analyses foregone conclusions, and builds
up formal results from acknowledged data. In this way he
attains certainty: but it is at the expense of catholicity, and
Logic becomes a science of particular, not of universal application. For the sphere, within which the universal science is
practical, is limited. Nor can it become more practical
without becoming special, and ceasing to be a pure science.
Whereas the advantage for science otherwise, and for the arts
generally, is precisely that they are special—that they are
complex, where complexity, in relation to circumstantial conclusions, is of use, and not complex, where complexity would
disconcert or confound. And the advantage for Style is
simply that the manifold details which aid its practical
exposition may be gathered into unity in a system whose
formal limits coincide with its material.

To the application of a science which, on such a general
view, promises a wider adaptation than even Logic, there can
be no direct objection, save under that class of objections
which founds on its special pretensions as an art. The sphere
which is most sanguinely claimed for it is, of course, the very
sphere from which it will be warned off most boisterously.

But the fact remains, that it will always be treated implicitly as a science. And not the circumstance of its being practical will supersede all scientific analysis, but analysis will be summoned to direct the bent of the practical issues; especially if a loose and flippant criticism is likely to prevail, and train it into a low and sterile order of performance. Under ordinary conditions, a subject is cultured theoretically because it is obscure: not comporting with the ease and extent of its practice, or not tallying with the results which might be expected from what already is presumed of its elastic powers, or from the forging ahead of kindred subjects. And if it remains obscure, it does so in spite of the counterworking culture. But where the analysis applied to it is superficial, not merely is the first of these cases reversed, but both are reversed. And the subject is not only cultured in spite of remaining obscure, but is obscured by the culture itself. The attitude of such a culture might perhaps be expected to be hostile to a more decisive analysis, the tendency of which is inevitably to supersede the other where it is narrow, and to amend it where it is false. And all the more, that in such a case it tends to dissipate the *feeling* of satisfaction with partial principles accepted as universal, and subordinate principles assumed as ultimate and fundamental. But the nature and beauty of the theme are sufficiently a corrective of any such illiberal reception. It is always an advantage, when it is possible to shift the reproach which may attach to the manner in which a subject is treated upon the subject itself as necessitating that treatment. Especially is it an advantage, when the attractiveness of the subject will neutralise the odium which might otherwise settle upon the particular mode of the examination. Most of all, however, when the general

opinion is deeply prepossessed in favour of the question, as
being of an interest so directly practical as that which is
⊤ inseparable from Style even under the most abstruse mode of
investigation.

It is well for literary criticism, nevertheless, that it should
be fortified in this way against vulgar misconceptions, whether
of a popular cast or of a quasi-philosophic. Its adaptability
for scientific purposes is indeed, to a certain extent, a reason
why it should not be cultivated, in spite of the concurrent
interest attaching to it; and why a collision arises between
the speculative bias and the practical. For here is a matter
coming under the eye of the ordinary reader every day, and in
so far qualifying him for a speculative interest in it in spite of
himself. Yet, on the other hand, his very familiarity with it
may, in spite of itself, and to the same extent, be a disqualification. The general question, however, with regard to the
treatment of such a subject in such a fashion, becomes really a
question of the *right* to treat it scientifically. Now apart from
the fact that a disgrace attaches to a science undeveloped,
similar to that which attaches to an individual or a nation
that is undeveloped, it is to be observed, that it is not
the absolute minimum of capacity which is addressed,
but only those are addressed, for whom possibly the theme
has attraction and intelligibility. A scientific treatment,
besides, is its own justification. It is nothing more than
an accurate examination of a mass of facts, directly or
indirectly in subordination to the highest known principles.
It can only be shown to fail, therefore, by a reference
to its own criterion, and by being detected to be *not* scientific,
i.e. not accurate, however pretentious in phrase;—and in so
far as it is inaccurate and pretentious, it is also culpable,

because discrediting sound terms and principles. As to the reader, he need not feel insulted by the assumption of his ignorance on the part of the critic. That ignorance on this particular subject is accidental. And the critic reciprocally pledges himself to give his most polite attention, at that date when the reader shall find it convenient to enlighten *him* on any subject he may chance to be ignorant of. Being a poor man, he will naturally wish to learn how to make money. Being an honest man, he will wish to have an insight into the way of making it fraudulently; the more especially that, being also inoffensive, he is disposed to find out how he can render himself obnoxious to society and to the law. And since he is farther a person of refinement, he will be seized with a desire to know upon what minimum scale of luxury a prison discipline allows a man to live. There is, in fact, no limit to the amount of theoretical information which may be supplied in this way; unless, of course, the reader demurs to such insinuations, as impertinently seeking to exalt his erudition at the expense of his honesty. Be it so: let the reader be as ignorant of these subjects as he is of the laws of literary criticism; and let it be equally an insult to his honesty to suppose him acquainted with these laws when he is not. But because the critic does not insult the reader in assuming his ignorance, he is not bound to insult him by assuming his incapacity. He dare not do so, indeed, when presenting to him for his profit, in a systematic form, what in any other would be meaningless. No pillar of fine proportions exists but what may be broken and pulverised; with a difficulty, moreover, in pulverising, corresponding to the difficulty of chiselling into shape. But the lessons which might be taught regarding the relations of angle and mass, etc. are not to be learned *after* the process of disintegration—else the sea-beach is the befitting spot for instruction.

The superficial treatment which is popularly decreed to Style, is sometimes decreed to it also by pure science. Thus it is that, under certain aspects, philosophic thought generally is repudiated by science, as attaining by mere brain-carpentry to a visionary stateliness of proportion, while it is buffeted by the populace for a proficiency that is gained only at the expense of its being communicable. All mental activity, indeed, is justly at a discount with exact thinkers, where it does not yield accurate results. It is only by irreflective persons that such rare inaccuracy is tolerated as that of an analyst, who, having enumerated all the facts (perhaps four or five) which come under a certain classification, adds, "these and a score of others," when his enumeration is simply complete. If undetermined in cases where the channel is so clearly marked out for him, is he likely to be less so, when his survey is partial or confused from the very outset ? Philosophy itself is the first to sneer at such bungling. At the same time the case may appear to it only normal in the circumstances, and inevitable under a critical *régime*. And that it does not sneer in this particular instance, may be owing to the fact that it has already recorded its formal disapprobation of the entire critical method. While from analogy, therefore, philosophy might be expected to support criticism, we must not be discomfited if it should withdraw its support, just at that point where the interests of the two cease to be common, and repudiate connection with it in its peculiar extensions, if not *in toto*, as cherishing principles incompatible with its own. The more the two orders of effects are studied, however, the more will it be seen that they resemble each other; and the

more will the thinking appear rustic and provincial, which
sets down the facts of literary science as trivial, and its principle as nugatory. And since the relations under which such
a charge may be substantiated are these two—(1) of the possibility of certain effects being *analysed*, and (2) of the possibility of their being *communicated*, it is in these relations that
the validity of a scientific criticism is most happily vindicated.

1. The case suggests itself as to the decomposition of rhetorical effects being possible. Sensibility being granted, the
question arises as to whether it is transformable into logical
propositions. A question so simple might be met by a reference to Art, as a branch of culture whose practical rules found
on effects which are first experienced in the sensitivity and
then brought into system—were it not that the reference
might be considered insufficient. For it might be argued that
the results in that section, in so far as they are parallel, are
due to quackery or self-delusion, or at least are equally unintelligible as to principle. Now the distinctive medium is the
same for both—a self-consciousness that yields faithfully, on
the one hand, to the impressions of sensibility, and readily,
on the other, to the pressure of the analytic intellect, when it
insists upon these impressions being reproduced. The part of
the intellect, therefore, is to suggest the alternative possibilities that might separately, or in combination, have effected
certain results. On equating and confronting these with the
reproduced sensibility, it will be declared which it is that has
been the sole or chief agent. Sometimes this takes place by
a positive and immediate decision. Sometimes, under a less
lively self-consciousness, it is brought about by the rejection
one after another of all the alternatives except those which

are to be received as having instigated the result. The alternative (if it is a single one) may happen to be indifferent, and
may refuse to give any positive token of its having operated.
Yet if the others shew positive signs of dissent, there is sufficient reason, in the circumstances, for accepting it as the
influential agent.

Such is the rationale of these effects, which (other things
equal) will shew themselves in exact proportion to the subtlety
of the investigator. And where no such results are found, we
simply infer, not the inviolability of the effects, but the inep-
titude of the analysis. That the presumed sensibility in any
individual case is great, in proportion to the meagreness of its
antecedents (as published through the scientific examination),
argues not that the sensibility is more, but that the critical
faculty is less. The very vagueness of exaltation with which
the critic colours his exposition, so far from testifying to the
exceptional degree of his susceptibility, may be simply the
exponent of his obscurity regarding it. What is possibly an
over-estimate of the delicacy of his individual impressions, can
never become the measure of the real subtlety of the impressions. For an excess of sensibility in regard to certain effects,
being purely subjective, is irrelevant to any purpose of philosophic analysis. It is with an objective sensibility, allowing
for the collation of one man's impressions with those of
another, that the science is concerned. Of two analysts, therefore, his conclusions will have most weight, who has inter-
preted his impressions most thoroughly. A critic may be very
modest, as well as very honest, in declaring that the facts with
which he occupies himself are too subtle for explanation. But
he is certainly a nincompoop, if he does not see that that
invalidates not in the least the chances of their being ex-

plained, except in so far as it is a fatal disqualification of himself, in point of that which is his sole recommendation in the matter. His assurances do not kill anybody but himself; they do not frighten, much less wound people of ordinary respectability. The sole exponent of sensibility is analytic power. That analysis meets the sensibility, therefore, is no lowering of *it*, but is an expansion of the parallel energy of the analytic intellect. Refuse the mind power to analyse, and you degrade it without exalting the sensibility. Admit this power, and you exalt it without degrading the sensibility. But the secret is that the indefiniteness of the sensibility (if it *is* indefinite) can only be shewn by at least *assuming* that it may be overtaken by analysis. It is either to be analysed, or not. If it is, this is all that is demanded. If not, then instead of the sensibility remaining simply at a point beyond the limits at which it may be pounced upon by science, it will be seen to mount indefinitely higher; since the more the analysis expands, the subtler will be the sensibility if after all it evades it, and the greater the indefiniteness of that of which confessedly the analysis has not been able to bring back any account.

The first alternative is the one to be concurred in for less speculative reasons. Not merely on a sentimental view, such as that of slighting the subtlety of the human mind in one sphere for the sake of magnifying it in another—which is fallacious as regards the first and futile as regards the second; nor because it is superficial to suppose that a study of the mind, in any even of its most barren sections, can be dismissed superficially; nor because the division of effects into those which may be treated analytically, and those which may not, is arbitrary, making a distinction of kind, where there is only

warrant for one of degree; but because the theory as to fact
is so erroneous; and to adopt the other correspondingly a
necessity, from the impulse not so much to embrace what is
psychologically true, as to reject what is psychologically
absurd. /The sensibility, we will assume, has yielded to certain effects, and in yielding has conformed to them. But it
could not thus have conformed to them, except by conforming
to their principles, under an intellectual guidance more or less
subconscious; which principles of guidance are exactly those
which it is the cue and the duty of the analysis to define.
Nor again, if the principles which underlie the sensibility are
not evasive, are they at least so anomalous as to interfere with
scientific completeness. They only appear anomalous to a
critic who either overlooks significant data, or else, having
already confused the data by a false classification, naturally
ascribes to them, by way of heterogeneousness, what is due to
the inconsistency of the method. Ultimate difficulty of this
order in science there need be none: so much barricade, so
much material for scaffolding. Finally, therefore, the investigator need not be confounded by any multiplicity of details,
in rising to the principles that will enable him to set and
view them in their proper relations. The same complexity is
common to all other sciences. It does not operate in the way of
baffling artistic insight; but is the indispensable condition of
artistic culture, and of a culture that is extended in proportion
as the details are numerous.

2. The distinctions which the theorist on Style has to deal
with present themselves first in the way of art, of art passive
and intuitive or perceptional; they are next received by science,
and their principles explicated; and finally they issue again
in the form of art, but this time of art active and militant,

ministerial and didactic. In this process science has a
double function, reposing on an organic connection, first,
between the actual sensibility of the investigator and his
analytic capacity, and secondly, between the analytic recep-
tivity of those he addresses and their potential susceptibility.
It is with Style in this latter relation that the second problem
is concerned, viz., as to the possibility of culture.

The instructor has to see and point out not merely abstract
varieties of expression, but these varieties under a limited
number of relations as ultimately good or bad. Hence the
farther classification of effects into those (1) which he along
with his readers'sees as bad or good, (2) those which he sees,
but which they do not see, and (3) those which they see, but
which he does not see, i.e. those which he sees them to see
through a medium of fallacy or distortion. From the collision
which may ensue between his sensibility and theirs, the
dilemma arises:—on the one hand, it is needless to put in a
scientific form what is already recognised as practical truth,
and, on the other, what is not recognised, since that confessedly is transcendental or contradictory. For either the result
which he seeks to establish is within the reach of the pupil,
in which case it is useless to harp upon it; or else it is out
of his reach, and there is no common ground to go upon.
Now, on a coarse estimate, it is quite possible to speak
of certain effects as being perceptible to the learners in
common with their instructor. But identically the same
effects will not be perceptible to each, or to all in the
same degree. A will represent an order of effects appreciable only in part to some who appreciate B, a different order
of effects, or a higher order like C; and so by permutation all
through—points seen by some in common with the expositor

being missed by those who are more at home in other sections.
Some effects, therefore, there will always be repugnant to some
among the learners, prior to the philosophic explanation. But
besides this distinction, and apart altogether from the manifest
value of holding in a precise form (with increased security for
its practical application and for acquiring facts that move to the
music of similar principles) what otherwise must be held indefinitely, it is to be observed, that the novice demands for his
satisfaction a systematic rationale that indirectly shall confirm
or correct the impressions which previously he may have
formed. A rationale of such a kind has this value for the
tyro, not merely that he may know what is right or wrong in
the cases that are specified, but that he may decide to what
extent his standard has been just. And for this purpose he
requires in a formal treatise—which is supposed to transcend
at least the hints of conversation and of desultory criticism—
something more than the mere expression of a casual coincidence between himself and the critic. The needs of the case
are not met by a simple statement, that such and such a
passage is beautiful, etc. The vagueness of the assertion may
really be in league with the reader's falser taste to deceive
him, even in cases where, if specific reasons had been alleged,
they might have been repudiated, and the plea resting upon
them dispelled. A more definite statement would be made in
describing the passage as luminous, etc. But the objection to
the use of metaphorical equivalents is not thereby removed.
Practically, indeed, such a term may be definite enough for
the reader. But this can only be through the distinct logical
meaning which he has already attached to it.

A certain number of technical equivalents is thus presupposed as known to the student, even in cases where his views

harmonise with those of the preceptor. Where the latter,
however, is concerned to put the matter so as to provide for a
rapprochement, in the event of being misunderstood, he will
do his best fully to explicate his meaning. In cases, therefore, where his sensibility is contradictory or transcendental,
it clamours most of all for a scientific exposition. A metaphorical expression may be not only vague, but sometimes
unintelligible or paradoxical. To say, for example, that the
following definition is brilliant in a literary sense, is only
puzzling to the mind whose preconceptions of brilliance are
those of vivid metaphor, or racy personality, etc. " I use the
term negative condition as equivalent to the term *conditio sine
qua non* and both in the scholastic sense. The negative condition of x is that which being absent x cannot exist; but
which being present x will not *therefore* exist, unless a positive ground of x be co-present. Briefly—if not, not: if yes,
not therefore yes." When it is explained, however, that the
brilliance, on which stress is laid in this instance, is that of
condensation (by means of the most exquisite simplicity), the
synthesis of the two ideas becomes apparent. And a new
flexion is given to the idea of brilliance generally, under
which rapidity of execution is subsumed as an element of
rhetorical prowess, and therefore to be admired, and of effect,
and to be imitated. The figurative expressions, regarding
which a sufficient definiteness of opinion prevails, are too
general for the specification which criticism needs, as well as
by far too limited in their number. The public, for the most
part, conceits itself upon the recognition of the principle that
reasons must be assigned for maintaining any proposition. It
does not take much pains, at all events, to remember that
it is specific, not general reasons, which constitute a valid

ground of *authority;* and especially that this is the only
ground of authority. It is too obstinately or too languidly
content with phrases, which seem comprehensive, but simply
are vague, neither ultimate, on the one hand, nor specific, on
the other. Most of all, in reference to literary art, it needs
peremptorily to be reminded that every statement which is not
countersigned by distinct reasons is to be received only as a
personal assurance. Individual opinion is virtually private
opinion, though it were published in folio, and had run through
fifty editions. There are occasions, doubtless, on which an
unsupported assertion is quite allowable. But these stand in
a class by themselves. And the reader need not hesitate to
reject an assurance in cases where the point at issue is strictly
critical—*i.e.* admitting a *balance* of reasons, and calling for a
determination to one side or the other—especially in the
absence of any indirect support given to it by a general
scientific cast of treatment. In the casual absence of such
reasons he will respect the critic for his general judiciousness
(as shown in the accuracy of his explanations, and the tact
with which he selects and varies his examples, etc.), and
give him the reflex benefit and prestige of any success which
he has fairly won. For the critic, however, to take advantage
of his acknowledged status, for bullying the reader into com-
pliance regarding one solitary fact of which he cannot furnish
the rationale, is the vulgar trick of the electioneering landlord,
in a political contest, who uses his influence to bias the votes
of his tenants.

The sensibility of the communicator is, then, we will
assume, virtually transcendental: since that is a condition for
its being of use to others. The remaining condition, which is
that it shall be intelligibly communicated, is fulfilled in its

scientific exposition, in so far as that is a guarantee of its *unequivocal* expression. Anything more, indeed, would be finical or officious; in the spirit of the martinet or the propagandist. We have thus in sensibility, acting concurrently with analysis, guaranteed the abnegation of all benefit to be derived from the monopoly of any faculty of æsthetic perception, except in so far as its results are incommunicable. And to that extent there is a warrant for individual sincerity; since it is clearly not for the interest of any one to exhibit nakedly for imitation effects, which constitute indefeasibly the ground of a certain superiority on his part. Not that such a practice is necessarily disinterested. What the analyst aims at may be simply the advertising of his own peculiar mode of expression. But it is clear that strict analysis, so far from lending itself to promote that abuse, is hostile to it. Since the moment the critic supplies the rationale of certain effects (to whomsoever they may belong), he places the reader in a position to appraise them. It is precisely in the absence of a scientific valuation that impertinent collusion is possible on the part of the writer with his own individuality,—and a rhapsody on the art and its divine principles; which art and which principles naturally find their illustration in the jackanapes himself who commends them.

For his own sake, therefore, the writer is bound to supply a rationale that shall tally with the results of each artistic perception, and to free himself from the reproach of an exposition too servile in its glorification of a limited or spurious sensibility. Besides, his appreciation of effects, being possibly out of proportion to his executive power, may not have sufficient indirect testimony in the latter to win for it the respect which virtually it might deserve. On the other hand,

though his executive power may be considerable, it may be
partial; and narrow, in so far as it may be imitable. He is,
consequently, bound to show that he has a wider appreciation
of what is beautiful in expression than is registered in his
own practice. The contradiction might quite well arise, of
an analyst with inferior executive power, who yet shows a
greater knowledge of effects, not on account of his superior
analytic perception (which might easily happen), but on
account of his wider sympathy with artistic effects, than
another of greater intensive susceptibility. And a methodical
analysis is thus demanded, not merely as a means of the
proper interpretation of sensibility to the reader, or of recon-
ciliation between two hostile modes of artistic perception,
but through a blunt necessity, as the only test of artistic insight, whether existing in connection with executive sensibility, or not.

It scarcely needs to be said that the sort of rationale which
is here contemplated, is in every case a passive rationale; and
that critical science repudiates the conjuring up of factitious
reasons, as on a level with the practice of the auctioneer who
is paid on commission. It may be added that the philosophic
method is the one to be adopted by the critic, were it for no
other purpose than that of self-defence. The tendency of most
readers is, on the one hand, to agree on indifferent matters
with a critic who agrees with their opinions on other points;
and, on the other hand, to be ill-disposed on indifferent points
to a critic who generally disagrees with them. It is his
dignity as a critic which the scientific method secures; since
it enables him to free himself, in the one instance, from the
charge of having failed through his own weakness or bad
taste, and, in the other, of having succeeded merely through

favouritism. Finally, it is the tendency of the method to lower the apparent transcendence of the effects which are explained. An effect, unanalysed at two removes, is as transcendent to explication, and, prior to explication, is confounded under the same category of transcendence, as one at twenty removes. The critic is not in all cases, therefore, anything so very portentous in the matter of sensibility. Nor is he interested in concealing that many of his supposed new effects are only original, because for the first time formally stated, or explicated in new relations to each other, or from having been casually overlooked in a field that potentially is open to all, or having been perceived under circumstances of accidental facility yielded by proficiency in kindred sciences.

As to the actual results arising in any particular instance from the attempted transmission of the sensibility, it is clear that no absolute maximum can be guaranteed, even under a scientific process. A man whose natural sensibility is unequal in keenness to his intellect will by his unassisted efforts be unable to rise in the appreciation of artistic beauties. Yet so great potentially is the energy of the human susceptibility, acting in connection with the pure intellect, that when the ' rationale of the effects is explained to him (which rationale he could not have devised, simply because for him the effects did not exist), the sensibility will mount towards the point at which he has apprehended the other. And if it moves upwards by a fraction, the expedient is justified of colleaguing with it the analytic intellect; since without such a confederate, even under the contemplation of the sublimest models, the sensibility would not have travelled by that fraction towards the point which, in spite of its weakness, it has reached. In the converse case, the sensibility being

c

great as the analytic force is small, it is the former which
acts by way of stimulus to the latter. The result in this
instance is that of a proper discipline. For the untutored
sensibility, which is apt to be partial and to run riot in
extremes, science points out severer beauties, and beauties
simpler and plainer in their subordinate value.

It is essentially a corollary from this, and in keeping with
the whole tenor of the discussion, that the scientific method
is the invariable regulator and guide, whether for the
development of a sympathy with art where it is rudimentary,
or for the moderating of it where it is in excess. The method
of the instructor is not always positive, but often negative;
though always for the sake of some positive result. And
that this discipline of his does not necessarily travel from a
lower degree to a higher will counterbalance the objection
which may be raised against the method on the score of
elevating commonplace to the rank of genius, and so
degrading genius to the level of what is too easily to be
reproduced. This objection may now be added as supplementary to the other two.

3. The more transcendental the effect that is to be communicated, there is the greater necessity that it shall be
explicitly communicated: but the more explicitly it is communicated, the more chance will there be of its becoming
mechanical. Now what the method has to do is not to work
the lowest sensibility immediately, or even ultimately, up to
the highest—any more than it has to do with training the
dray-horse into the racer. What it aims at is a proficiency
from stage to stage, and from an initial stage in each case
to a final stage proportioned to the latent capacity of the
individual. The proficiency which it seeks to establish is

mechanical, in so far as it is easy and complete. But it is just on that account organic; since the effects are only reproducible in so far as they involve discrimination, and the discarding of vicious and less pertinent alternatives. Nor can that happen without the power to apprehend that this or that turn of thought under formation is or is not allowable on the score of relevance. What took place in analysing the presupposed sensibility is now taking place conversely in the application by the sensibility of what has been given to it through the presupposed analysis. When, therefore, a writer shows that he discerns what, in certain circumstances, is or is not relevant, he must be admitted to be in possession of the principle—a principle that being continually more under control works more rapidly, and therefore more organically, as manifested in its power to vary the form of expression; making easy what it holds, and making easy in order to hold. Otherwise, there is nothing of the nature of a *nostrum* in this scientific treatment, any more than of encouragement to a quavering and paralytic imitation of the more sublime effects.

In so far as the scientific method is the true method both of attaining and expounding the rationale of literary beauties, any illustration of its principle is not more a vindication of it than a condemnation of every other. Properly speaking, it is not vindicated, but freed from misapprehension. Since its merit is not distinguished from the merit of any other method, in the same way as homœopathy might be vindicated by one physician as against allopathy by another. It is not opposed to any

other as a more catholic to a less catholic, a more dignified
to a less dignified, a more effective to a less effective.   It
is blankly the only method; and beside it every other is
false.   No absolute vindication of it, therefore, is needed, and
no formal condemnation of any other.   The final objection,
however, is not one that applies to it as contradistinguished from possible rival methods—the other two do
apply to it in that sense—nor does its being rebutted
imply anything against them.   That objection is one that
might be brought against any art, and amounts to the
charge against the art that it is too practical—which is no
objection whatever, but a clumsy compliment.   The only
objection, in fact, on that score would be the second, viz.
that it is *not* practical; which the method evades by
enabling learners to reproduce, and, where that is impracticable, to appreciate, effects; distributing a greater
excellence in expression generally, and an increased appreciation of effects that are not imitable.

What concerns finally the positive results of the theory
of Style—its practical relations to other sciences—may be
summarily indicated.

1. For Philosophy generally it may be regarded as a
special introduction, like Logic and Grammar, either as
preliminary or complementary to these.   It is quite legitimately a propædeutic, since it contains a special discipline.
The other relations which it has to philosophy — its
secondary relation, as illustrating in its own details the
principle of philosophy, and its final relation, as possibly an
integral moment of philosophy, and having in and for
philosophic science an inseparable significance, as itself the
principle of *Critique*—do not concern us at this moment.

Psychology in general might be expected to reflect upon the science of literature a light, and that no intermittent light. But so much more chance is there of finding recurrent phenomena—apart from all resorts to cross-illumination from *abnormal* phenomena, which of themselves induce confusion—imbedded in literary expression, that there is more likelihood of literary science reflecting light upon psychology. Not otherwise did Logic stand in relation to psychology, as an offshoot from it, in certain respects, and derivatively an exponent of mental operations in spheres that showed themselves by no means so amenable to the laws of pure psychology as the facts of literature. The science of Style stands side by side with that of Logic ; and mediates between the abstract intellect and pure sensibility, which in turn is bounded by the anomalies that scowl and gibber on the outskirts of Medical Psychology.

2. Within the sphere of psychology Art in general falls itself to be treated. And the science of Style, just in proportion as its principles are stated with authority, cannot fail to reflect a light upon the arts, any more than they reciprocally upon it. Especially it must add its testimony to that of Painting (an art that is infinitely further advanced), in regard to the analysis of Music, which, in so far as melody and the other concrete phenomena are concerned, is scientifically a blank. In this relation it is an isolated science, not organically connected with fundamental principles of psychology.

But more decisively, as connected with those effects which appeal to the eye, on the one hand, and to the ear, on the other, literary science is central to all artistic criticism. It is not merely one among the branches of art, and (since it falls to be taken into account in any complete survey of art), indispensable to scientific completeness. It comes to affect and modify the general conception of art, which, being true only in so far as it takes notice of all the varieties and in their leading ramifications, is headlong in acknowledgment of this its most catholic form. Literary science must, therefore, radiate an influence upon art that practically will make itself felt, not merely in the suggestion of individual relations to the artist, under the rapprochement of the total science, but in moulding the judgments of artists of one class with regard to those of another. Supreme pity it is, when jealousy, the jealousy of irritation to inferiors, and of animosity to men of equal or of higher powers, is permitted to stifle the genial sympathy which should belong to art. The landscape painter knows himself, on the ground of high conception and of delicate execution, to be above the house-painter. But he feels much more inclined to sympathy with the latter, when his spirit is professionally roused: and that not because, but in spite of the fact that the acknowledgment of the nexus between the two arts is not so much due to catholic sentiment as to a refined intellectual perception. Even if such jealousy were the rule, however, among artists of the same class, the widening of the boundaries of art, showing the inosculation of the various arts with each other, by extending indefinitely the opportunities for jealousy instead of fostering bad feeling is more likely to do away with it altogether.

3. There is one sphere, finally, for which, as a preliminary study, the theory of Style is less of a scientific luxury, and more of a necessity, that, viz. of literary criticism; for which it cannot fail to supply a rich fundus of operative principles. Owing to its scientific cohesion, it has an advantage in in-

fluencing the other branches of literary art that is not possessed by unsystematic criticism. And from isolated criticism—the criticism that is applied to separate works or fragments of works—it is still further distinguished by being removed above the element of personality; and of personality in both its forms. In the first instance, it is spared the temptation, or the necessity, of criticising individual writers. And in the second, it evades such circumstances of the critic's own personality as the want of space, the necessity of a treatment that shall be popular, diffuse, and without regard to any scientific basis, and more specially, a position on a staff of writers, where, the general tenor of thought being prescribed, the critic is not entirely free, or where, if its tenor is promiscuous, he finds little reason for preserving consistency.

Absolutely central to the sciences which control literary criticism Style must always be. Psychological distinctions manifest themselves here most appreciably At no point, therefore, is its culture unattended by a reflex illumination of these sciences, which present such Pacific expansions of novelty for speculation. Itself forms the first in the order of analytical development; the second being that general science which has for its main divisions Poetry, Philosophy, etc. The third is the science of Rhetoric, the synthesis and application of both; which may be viewed, in the latter respect, as a special science, in the former, and by way of comprehending the others, as equivalent to the theoretical generally in literary science.

The sciences in this triad, while they are complementary to each other, and admit of a natural sequence in their

treatment, admit of being treated independently of one
another. At the same time they all acknowledge the following method of division, (1) as a body of facts shown in their
scientific cohesion, (2) as a body of principles shown in their
ultimate significance, and (3) as a body of truth shown in its
relations to praxis. Accordingly the immediate science
divides itself as, in the first place, the Analytic of Style, in
the second, the Logic, and in the third, the Synthetic of Style.
With regard to which partition it is to be noted, in the first
place, that the nomenclature is ambiguous, in so far as the
method is concerned, that being in the Logic as much analytic
as in the technical Analytic itself. In the second place, the
Logic, with which this volume is engaged, usurps the place of
the Analytic ; the order is transposed; the inversion being a
matter of scientific propriety and of convenience. The de-
ductive portion, however, which the Logic represents, founds
exclusively on the inductive, represented by the Analytic (by
which indeed it was suggested). Does the Logic, therefore,
contain more or less than is warranted by the other, it errs,
certainly by inadvertence, possibly by fallacy. The Analytic
of Style, along with the Synthetic, or third and final section,
is for the time withheld. Not unnaturally the speculative
treatment by itself may seem to, exhibit a certain heartless-
ness of abstraction. And to exhibit Style abruptly in its
unity, its principle, is doubtless to make it somewhat abstruse for the general reader. Nevertheless it is here, in any
event, that the supreme nisus must be made. The Analytic
is only secured, whether by anticipation or not, through a
rationale of the fundamental principles of Style in their
ultimate coherence—after which to pursue the theme into its
separate sections is mere undress and holiday scramble.

THE LOGIC OF STYLE.

CHAPTER I.

OF STYLE GENERALLY.

Section I. Of Expression Generally.

1.

THAT is a natural distinction which obtains between Thought
as it exists in the mind *per se*—Thought pure and essential—
and Thought as formulated in Expression. The distinction
is natural in so far as it is first fundamental, and secondly
obvious. And it holds not merely of Thought generally, but
of Thought in particular. It is true, therefore, of every result
of mental activity in which Thought and Expression coexist;
what is contemplated being, not an order of cases in which
the antithesis basks between two quasi-equivalent terms, of
which the one is a spurious or precarious form of the other,
but the universal case, in which it glares between the two
relations of any term, considered in the one view as Expression, and in the other as Thought.

No antithesis can be conceived more universal, since it is
an antithesis whose principle is involved in every expression. No principle the most universal can be expressed

which does not involve *it*. But this is not the entire truth.
It has a distinctive mode of involution, superadded to the
other and arising from it. Lord S. holds that Mr. Y. is
the proper person to fill a vacant office of state. That he
means what he says is one thing; but that it implies something else in addition is another, as is clear from this, that
his assertion gives offence to Lord T., who presumably
holds another view, since he contradicts the view of Lord
S. And he seconds his contradiction by the avowal that
Mr. X. is the person for the situation. But having avowed
so much, he likewise *implies* (what is painfully disagree-
able to Lord S.) that Mr. Y.'s claims are not for a moment
to be put in comparison with those of his respected friend
Mr. X. And if Lord S. cherishes animosity against Lord T.
it will be not so much because it was asserted that Mr. X.
was worthy of the place, as because it was implied that his
candidate and *protégé* Mr. Y. was not. If, indeed, you
accept the expression of favour shown for his client by
each of the noble lords, you will be convinced that both
ought to have the place; but if you accept his implication,
you will see that both are equally unfit. Wherever, therefore, a principle is expressed, it is not involved. And conversely, where it is involved, it is not expressed. Now the
peculiarity of our principle—that of the distinction between thought and expression—is that the truth which *it*
expresses is at the same moment also involved or implied.
For since every principle that is expressed involves this
principle, and this principle is now expressed, it follows
that this principle involves this principle, *i.e.* involves
itself. Q. E. D. Itself is involved by itself, and is itself an
illustration of itself. The implication in the case we con-

sidered first is not, of course, the same in kind with the latter implication, which is more strictly an involution. It was introduced merely by way of oblique illustration. On reading a proposition, its implication (in the proper sense) is the first to occur to any one. A higher reflection is needed to suggest to itself the relation which in addition it involves—the antithetic relation of thought and expression—as well as the universality of that involution; and still a higher to perceive that this is not merely an abstract relation, but a concrete—a fact coincident with its own principle, and a subject amenable to its own laws.

COR.—No distinction is held with the most lively chance of being realised, until it is seen in a concrete case. And generally such an illustration is hardest to bring to light, when it is most necessary that it should be forthcoming to vindicate the principle—in many cases to enforce it, in some even to make it intelligible. In this instance there is no such difficulty. The principle of the distinction is universal. Allowing for the extreme of abstruseness and complexity, it provides also for the extreme of simplicity. A simple thought, therefore, is as completely an illustration of the antinomy in its relation to expression as a complex.

2.

The independence in the mutual relations of thought and expression is one that practically holds true only of thought, and for expression is quite nugatory. For the latter the distinction is purely an abstract, not an operative distinction. For the former, too, it is only practical within certain limits. The activity of thought must, as a rule, be enhanced and multiplied by permitting a formula, and with a result whose

magnitude is often inversely as the force employed. I do not
mean simply in such a case as that of an intellectual revolution, whose influences radiate through a purely literary
medium; since that suggests too advantageously for illustration the inseparable element of expression, and its value
as a medium—but in an order of cases where both elements
are combined in by no means a similar degree of harmony
and purity. In a political revolution, for example, there is
one constant and animating element of *thought*, whether propagating itself by mere animal contagion of sympathy, or by
sympathy of a more intellectual type. Which element is
radically the same with that in the other case, and its conditions of success are essentially the same, and its mode of
working is in principle the same. The prominent fact in this
instance, as in the other, is the *communication* of the influence, which again we will suppose to have radiated from
a solitary individual. Thus between the origin and the
result, the obscure origin and the vast result, there is, if we
look forward, merely the fact of a silence; if we look back-
ward, merely the fact of a silence negated. Simply in his
own person the initiator could not have affected what, by
this negation of his silence, he has virtually effected. Otherwise he must single-handed have done the whole work,
manned the batteries, marched in a body to the point of
attack, etc. And just in proportion as he discarded expression, would he become increasingly unable to fulfil his
mission, when it was becoming increasingly necessary that
he should fulfil it. The more thought is required, therefore,
the more does expression as a coefficient mount into importance. And if for thought, in certain relations, expression
is indispensable, much more is thought indispensable to

expression; since only in and through thought is expression possessed of a living and elastic energy.

1. Considered in their *ultimate* relation to each other, thought has a regulative value for expression. To say that expression has no significance apart from thought is the same thing as saying that it has no existence apart from thought: its very existence founds upon its being significant. For it is to be noted that this significance is not the figurative thing that is commonly represented by the term in relation to individual expressions. It is, in fact, the condition of their existence; which existence, in its turn, becomes the condition of the derived significance as popularly understood. The meaning of the symbol "brand," for instance, is for us that of a billet under consumption by fire, and reduced more or less to a smouldering red. So long as it preserves this form, every Englishman understands what is meant. But let the letters be transposed, so that they shall read "bnard," and instantly for us it becomes unintelligible. Its total significance has not disappeared, however; only its actual significance has disappeared. Its potential significance remains; its precise significance for us now consisting in this that it is *un*-intelligible, *i.e.* not directly and immediately significant. For the savage in the same way a very simple sign may produce discomfiture, as before something which he can easily reproduce, but which he cannot interpret. That discomfiture arises not more from ignorance than from knowledge; it being the special aggravation of the case that to his perception of the sign he adds so much acquaintance with the principle of signs generally, as to decide that this sign is not accidental, but for somebody has an obvious

interpretation that is denied to him.   The occasion of his
perplexity is the same with that of the art of the professional decipherer.   In the one case, however, the
possible significance of symbols mediates only to conscious recognition of ignorance, in the other to its removal.

2. It is upon thought that the positive and *immediate*
significance of every expression depends. / Expression has
no operative value, except as being the medium of propaga-
tion for thought ; a truth which holds particularly in relation to expressions connected in a series, since that depends
entirely upon the logical movement of the thought, and the
associations inseparably connected with each expression.
Of which express corroboration is found in the fact
(apparently irreconcileable with the principle) that a meaning may be gleaned from propositions whose terms are not
separately clear.   The onus of the weak terms has simply
been borne by the stronger, which, but for their own
integrity, must themselves have succumbed under the
extra responsibility.   The proposition has proved intelligible in spite of the casual unintelligibility of one of the
terms, not in spite of the rule which demands the intelligibility of all the terms.   Under the latter alternative the
meaning of the proposition as a whole would not have been
made out.   And very specially it is overlooked, in arguing
for the contradiction of the rule by this apparent exception,
that in the final result the word *is* intelligible ; what is
contemplated in the rule being that no term shall be
introduced which may absolutely withstand the plenary
power of a passage to interpret itself, a power of interpretation that extends even over its obscure members.   For
there is a separate reason why any superficial canon,

ordaining the exclusion of obscure terms, should be
suspended. What the familiar terms of the proposition are
commissioned to raise to their own status is invariably a
term that is not absolutely unfamiliar, but simply is not
yet quite explicitly comprehended. And what they do is
to ratify, under a specific collocation of ideas, what had
been left inchoate under other collocations, though pre-
pared by these successively for that ratification. It is
because the number of alternatives was limited, under
which the unknown term could be understood, that it has
been understood. And it is the other terms in the connection which have been exactly the agency (for I represent
them collectively, not individually as agents) in reducing
these alternatives from indeterminateness to an operative
and influential definiteness. That agency evidently is not
the one to be overlooked. And yet it is the agency that is
overlooked, in saying that the meaning has been reached
independently of the connection between expression and
thought. To deny the interdependence is in fact as
rational as, in the converse case, to complain of the want
of news in a public journal, in the forgetfulness of the
circumstance that one had previously gone the round of all
the contemporary papers within reach.

3. *Indirectly* thought is always present in expression.
This is what the mechanical reader chiefly misses—the
suggestiveness of certain collocations of thought. For
there is a very trenchant distinction between the man
who reads with just enough intelligence to surmount
the meaning of every proposition as it reached him,
and the man who reads with active intelligence sufficient
to explicate for himself the associations with which the

terms of a proposition may exalt and reflect its primary
significance.

> " She came to the village church
> And sat by a pillar alone ;
> An angel watching an urn
> Wept over her, carved in stone ;
> And once, but once, she lifted her eyes,
> And suddenly, sweetly, strangely blush'd,
> To find they were met by my own." [1]

The situation is infinitely natural—the evasive quiescence of the maiden, confronted by the eternal, aggressive
masculine gaze—for else how could the boy *know* that she
had lifted her eyes only once ?—and the disruption, in
which, through a mere gleam, a quiver, all is for *her*
undone, and the very quiescence has become for *him*
treacherously significant. But the circumstances, but the
associations—the fusion of sentiment at that exact point
where the spiritual merges into the sensuous—the intensity
of ritual suggestion, variously expounded by the solemn
agencies of the ceremonial, mystically by the organ,
articulately by the priest, and by the worshippers in a
murmured unison that is half mystical, half articulate—
confounded and overborne by the intensity of human passion,
that ought to be in antagonism to it, but *is* not, does not
strive with it, therefore, but leagues it subtly with itself,
and so helps to concentrate and amplify the sense of communion—a communion equivocal, and founding expressly
upon a truth equivocally applied, viz. Love — all this
perishes as in a vacuum to the careless reader. In this relation, therefore, he may legitimately be styled mechanical,
either from his want of the power of reflection, or from his

---

[1] From Mr. Tennyson's " Maud."

want of the power of attention, interfering with the natural
action of the other. Not that every passage will bear the
same stress of reflection. The difficulty often is to avoid
reflection. Indeed an evil motive in criticism, whether of
partiality for or against a writer, where it does not manifest
itself in tampering with the views expressed by him, will
manifest itself in tampering with the expression of these
views—in reading for profound what is superficial, and for
superficial what is profound. And the rationale of the fact
which is so vaguely expressed in saying that a man sees in
the writing of another more or less than there is to be seen,
is precisely this, that unduly he masses and brings into
relief, or fails duly to integrate and gather into a focus the
collateral suggestions of the text.

Cor.—No distinction more visionary could be drawn than
that which it might be attempted to draw between the
organic in expression and the mechanical. Such a distinction
(if it has any meaning at all, apart from that indicated in § 1)
can only take effect in relation to the movement of full-blown
propositions. Now it is here precisely that the power of
expression in the way of oblique suggestion is most valuable,
for reciprocally controlling and modifying the meaning of the
constituent terms in a proposition, so as to preserve its organic
unity. Let us, for instance, examine this proposition: "The
prejudices of society have not been found directly to aid its
progress." If we subtract the word "not" from the proposition, we shall have committed a most comprehensive
felony upon the tenor and direction of the thought. It ran
from east to west: we have made it run from west to east.
But if, reintroducing the "not," we expunge the word
"directly," we shall effect substantially the same result. The

well-being of a state would doubtless be increased, if that
malignity of prejudice were absent, which often springs from
local or individual rivalry.   Yet that may help to breed com-
petition and higher activity in branches of trade that else
might languish.   And so prejudice does not absolutely im-
pede the progress of society, but indirectly abets it. Other
flexions might be given to the proposition, such as that "immediately," or "finally," or "unconsciously," or "impalpably,"
or "paradoxically," or "naturally," "the prejudices of society
have been found to aid its progress."   But always another in-
flection is given to the sense.   Expressions the most contradictory, such as "paradoxically," and "naturally," may on
occasion be used indifferently; and expressions like "unconsciously" and "impalpably" (where the one is as it were
the specific form, the other the generic) may be substituted
for each other.   But there is no expression, however faintly
differing from another, for which, in precise writing, most
circumstances are not crucial in applying its distinction from
that other.

In regard to which it may be observed, that the new
specific terms that are continually being made do not tend to
supersede the old, any more than they do in the mind of the
individual writer—old terms revealing themselves to his mind
more explicitly and completely, and new terms filling up
lacunas in thought hitherto unsuspected. In both instances
the movement is universal, that of a tide, not of a wave. And
it is only by relation to the terms of older standing that the
new are enabled to maintain their position. The old is not
therefore indefinite, because the new happens to be specific,
nor the new incomplete, because the other is more universal.
The coarse and grotesque way of interpreting innovation in

expression is that all fresh terminology supersedes the ancient, and is useless; further that it tends unnecessarily to multiply terms, and is therefore harmful, which is precisely to say that the needle tends to supersede the chisel. Meantime the value of the needle generally consists in this, that it does *not* do every kind of work, and in particular that it is not available for the work to be done by the chisel. And to put a stop to the variation of terms before the proper limit, is not merely to suppress the immediate forms of variation, but the possible ramifications of these in arrear. For every new thought there must arise a corresponding expression. Nor can any other principle be laid down, by which the number of ideas shall be increased for every term from this limit to the abracadabra or ideal formula, which shall embrace explicitly the whole cycle of knowledge and being, the sum of things actual and possible. An economising of terms has no use apart from an economising of ideas. But such an expedient as that of diminishing the number of terms would never reduce the sum of ideas. If it could, it would do so wrongly. The only real economy that is possible in the matter is in the suppression of the riderless and supernumerary among terms. And so it is that economy is in exact harmony with the converse canon, viz. that every expression shall have its independent thought. To multiply expressions, therefore, for a single idea is not to enhance the chances of its being distinguished, but to defeat them; and in this case to violate the canon of reciprocity by sheer blankness of meaning, as in the other by sheer multiplicity of interconfounded association. Hence, and on both sides, the essential vice of modern slang; which may be described generally as the tendency, on the one hand, to elevate expressions drawn from

the vulgar quasi-professional classes, etc., and on the other to
degrade expression, by drawing into a comical quasi-figurative
reference terms of ordinary and even catholic significance.
Thus, on the one side, we have a purposeless multiplication
of terms for such acts as stealing, running away, etc., and on
the other, a burdening of certain terms, such as "governor"
and "lot" (e.g. "a queer lot" applied to an individual) with a
superfetation of meanings. This happens obviously within
limits. Since no possibility of leisure, no possibility of
malice, could ever enable an individual or a number of individuals to multiply terms for *every* thought; and no
possibility of indolence or of preoccupation can prevent men
from fitting up *most* of their ideas with an adequate terminology. But excesses and defects do exist more or less in
all languages to disturb the just equilibrium between the in-
novations of language and the stagnation of thought. In so
far as these *tend* to neutralise each another, thought is kept in
activity. Otherwise, in individual instances, they constitute
separate sources of imperfection—such as might be found in
polyandry superadded to polygamy.

3.

Expression is to be regarded as coinciding with thought;
but inasmuch as every thought (with certain obvious exceptions) is complex, a dual or *equivocal* relation arises for expression, that, viz., in which it corresponds wholly to the
thought, and that in which it corresponds to it only in part.
This happens constantly in composition, where terms are used
now in relation to their generic meaning, now in relation to
their specific. One may say, for example, that "curiosity led
a man to watch the movements of the celestial bodies,"

where he means simply "the desire of knowledge," dis-
engaged from the element of pettiness and gratuitousness
which is implied in the actual statement. Or again, he may
say that "the desire of knowledge induced a man to open
his friend's writing-case, and examine his correspondence,"
when he means curiosity. In the one instance he says too
much, in the other too little; and in both cases we know
analytically by how much, the measure of excess in the one
being identically the measure of defalcation in the other.
But the novelty is this, that it is by the very inaccuracy of
the statement that we are able to correct it, and by substituting the one reciprocal for the other to give our amended
version of the truth. The principle of specification has been
abused in the one case, and neglected in the other. But
virtually it has righted itself. And by way of compensation
its value now mounts into its place and is realized, when we
present the truth in its authorized form. Thus it happens
that expression may be represented in two aspects, under the
one of which it is exceedingly vague, and under the other
exceedingly definite. A charge of verbalism, for example, is
a charge of meaninglessness. And, on the other hand, expression is regarded as the seal and redundance of faithfulness
in all communication. The one founds upon the indisputably
arbitrary nature of signs considered in themselves, the other
on the indisputable teleologic value of signs. Convertibly
thought and expression are the same; a *virtual* coincidence
being secured, whether the expression is something more, or
less, or else, than the thought. But their coincidence may be
actual as well as merely virtual. And hence the relation of
expression to thought is equivocal.

If every term as it is met with in general writing were

to be understood always in its *special* incidence, and not
with reference to its proximate terms, its genus and
species, it would begin to fluctuate in its meaning; that
meaning would begin to be shared by other terms, and it
itself by degrees might (quite apart from the dialectical
tendency of language) drift into other relationships, and
become the bearer of successive associations widely differing
from each other. That, for the most part, the phrases in
present use have not yielded to such a tendency, is to be
ascribed to the fact of the counter-tendency to revert after
deflection to the original signification. These terms preserve in a double sense the consistency of language, both
in themselves, and for others, by acting as centres of
stability amid fluctuation. But occasionally they themselves fluctuate; and in so far language is elastic and not
rigid; as, with regard to the essentially unstable terms, it
is elastic, not ductile. It gains its virtual immobility by
seasonable fluctuation. But that literary effect varies, not
in relation to language alone, (and, for example, the very
contradictory expression of what one means is a form of
wit) and bears an equivocal relation through what is itself
essentially stable, may be illustrated from mathematics,
which hitherto has shown itself the most adamantine and
inexorable of standards. Fifty pounds are fifty for the
banker and for everybody. But the literary significance
of fifty is different from its financial. Three may be more
significant. But also fifty may be more significant than
three. This significance then is variable, and affronts
arithmetic, first by discarding its principle of proportion,
and, in the next breath, by coming back to it. But note how
for all that it is indebted to the arithmetical immobility.

For if the number fifty were not always the same, whether existing at a premium with regard to three, or at a discount, who could guarantee that the one, which had stood up with alacrity to discount the other, should not have transmuted itself into some third number when the time came for it to be discounted? The invariability of the number, therefore, which is the safeguard of the banker against embezzlement by his clerks, is precisely the safeguard of literary significance.

Cor.—Writing generally consists in a variation of the two styles of absolute precision and merely relative precision. And so long as that variation is preserved, it is to a certain extent indifferent in individual cases which style is observed. The ideal absurdity would be to use the generic and the specific as convertible where they are not, and to neglect using them as convertible where they are indifferent. To say, therefore, that it is indifferent which standard is used, does not imply that the privilege of having alternate standards is to be abused. A writer, from extreme prepossession or carelessness, may use a generic term for a specific, and *vice versa*; so as to bewilder his readers by ambiguity, or even absolutely to mislead them. In this case the alternative standard becomes simply pestilent. A second order of cases is that in which it is really indifferent, as to the sense, whether the expression is absolutely precise or not. Here there is a legitimate use of the standard as supplementary to the other. But thirdly, there are occasions on which this standard becomes virtually or even absolutely a complementary standard. Thus, for example—what suits eminently the elliptical method of poetical expression—it is so in the lines :—

> Like form in Scotland is not seen,
> Treads not *such* step on Scottish green—

a rare truism in itself, since notwithstanding that certain types
of gait might accompany certain types of figure, everybody
knows that no two men have the same shape and carriage.
But for that very reason it is seen that something more is
hinted than the truistic fact—a comparison within the comparison, and an expression of pre-eminent or paramount dignity
associated with form and step. Again the antithesis of the
idea may be employed to convey a transferred meaning. Thus
in the expression :—

> Fallen heroes want
> Yonder in heaven their crown of blessedness
> Till the last *bondsman* clasp unfettered hands
> O'er the last slaver whelm'd beneath the wave,

the word "bondsman" is taken to designate a special agent
in a significant circumstance, where *ex hypothesi* the individual
is no longer a bondsman. To such an extent does the principle of expression sublate itself in its literal form (and quite
apart from every metaphorical usage of terms) for a relative
and virtual intelligibility ; and in special cases by hinting the
substantial truth where more is expressed, by integrating it
where less, and by rectifying it where the reverse is expressed.

Section II. Of Style in its relation to Expression.

4.

Style is the Differential in Expression : and this, which
exhibits it in its most characteristic reference, is its scientific
definition.

In relation to Style, expression, which tends indefinitely
to extend or differentiate itself as regards thought, must be
assumed to have reached a limit. It is very clear that Style
is not the differential of expression, in the same way that

expression may be regarded as the differential of thought.
(1) Expression does not reach a limit in order to allow style
to take up the process of specification. Such a limit would
be arbitrary; and it would be unjust to expression to lay
down any terminus at which its distinctive principle was to
be superseded. (2) Style does not consist in stray specifi-
cations made by individual thinkers. That would be unjust
to itself. These casual terms can only show themselves in
obedience to the general laws of differentiation; and in so
far as they do that they belong to expression, not to style.
It is distinctly a proof of this (what might appear in direct
contradiction of it) that every expression in use at any
period must have been struck out by an individual. Since
precisely to the extent that it was necessary would it be
adopted, with a rapidity that would confound the individuality of the discoverer. Of innovation in terminology
only these four kinds are possible, (1) that which is required and is adopted, (2) that which is required but is not
adopted (not being published widely enough for immediate
adoption), (3) that which is not required but is adopted,
and (4) that which is not required and is not adopted. These
classes, however, reduce themselves to two, the first and the
last; since the other two tend to right themselves, and in
part by neutralising each other. Now (with regard to the
fourth) there are many terms that sprout up in the spor-
tiveness of correspondence, or in the heat and condensation
of journalism, that are literally ephemeral. And connecting
themselves with no catholic principle of expression, they
cannot be viewed as possibly approaching a thing so organic
as style. As to the terms of the first class, it is clear that
they are few, and can never serve as the exponent of a

writer's individuality. Besides, being engrossed by other
writers, they lose, except to the antiquary, any value as
having been originated by him; the very permanence of
literature, which guarantees the perpetuation of the term,
gainsaying its permanence as affecting our estimate of the
originator. It is to his use of the common items of expression that a man owes his individuality. The limit which
expression is assumed to have reached for style is not, therefore, a limit at which *innovation* in expression begins; which
would be to extend the limit that *ex hypothesi* is final. That
process is the very one which we must assume to have
ceased. For now the movement for style is precisely in the
opposite direction. Accordingly to differentiate expression
is obviously not to distribute it by diversification of individual expressions, but (3) to redistribute it, by combining and
unifying a variety of these under a definite idiosyncrasy.
The individuality in the one case is that of a fact, in the
other that of a person—of individuals as against individuals,
writers against writers, speakers against speakers. Formally
the principle of the one is variety, that of the other unity.
Only style tends also to differentiation in a mass, with a
resultant variety of styles proportioned to the variety of
individual expressions.

Cor.—The relation of style to expression is one of complete
interdependence. Expression being distinctively the basis of
the other, there is no point in its extension by which style
does not profit; being the sphere for the exhibition of style,
which raises the potential in expression to the actual, there
is no extension of style by which it does not profit. All that
is assumed is, therefore, a certain totality of expression.
Which totality, acting, in the second place, in combination

with psychological tendencies, is determined, in the third
place, to a known variation and recurrence of certain forms of
expression, forming in itself that totality of expression,
in its extent or intensity, which we call a man's style.
This is properly illustrated in the relation of the classical
and Saxon elements in the English language. It has
been shown (§ 2, p. 50) to be gratuitous and unscientific to
treat the former element as if by possibility it could supplant
the latter. Together they form a totality of expression, in
which generally (1) the Latin (as the typical exoteric element)
is the differential of the Saxon. "World" for example has its
definite significance, generally considered. But what of it in
special relations—in relation to totality as compared with its
own local sections? In that case it is "cosmopolitan." Or
what of it again by way of relation to the transcendent whole
of the universe, or as equivalent itself to that whole ? It then
becomes "sublunary," or "cosmical." And through the combination of these two elements it is that the genius of the
English nation is realised in that special literary form which
we call its "idiom." Out of that relation, however, arises
another, in which each element becomes a separate function,
or a separate aggregate of functions. Thus, roughly speaking,
the Saxon takes cognisance of facts, the Latin of principles.
More particularly, the Saxon is concerned with the domestic
and the catholic sensibilities (in a nation so keenly alive, on
the one hand, to the tendernesses, and, on the other, to the
sublimities of human sympathy as the English) and the Latin
with the abstract relations of things. Thus (2) in regard to
the totality of expression, each becomes a *co-differential* with
the other. Each represents a leading psychological distinction. Latin, as being the element which is *not* the vernacular,

and being superinduced upon the other (as the thinking of the
adult is superinduced upon the thinking of the child), becomes
valuable not for its being casually or immediately the negation of popular thinking, but positively for its catholic
precision, which is the cardinal test and necessity of a
scientific diction.   On the other hand, the virtue of our Saxon
lies in its simplicity, which is the necessity of a poetical
diction.   A writer's general bias will, therefore, be determined
by the proportion in which the two elements mingle in his
expression.   For evidently it *is* a proportion, in which neither
is found exclusively.   And hence (3) the Latin and the Saxon
become each *reciprocally* the differential of the other.   If, in
average use, these two elements bear a certain proportion to
each other, then evidently the writer who uses more Latin
than other people has that for the differentia of his literary
manner,—the quantity being supposed equal in all cases, he
will use less of the Saxon.   And similarly in the converse
case.   A more natural case, of course, is that of subvarieties in
these elements.   Thus, of two writers having a poetical and
philosophic diction, one has in addition a scientific bias; that
becomes his differentia, not, however, simply in relation to the
Latin compound, but to the whole complement of his expression.   The Saxon is still a co-efficient to discriminate
that complement from any other; what was expressed in
the previous instance by extent, being now represented by
intensity, as measured by recurrence.

5.

Since Style is to be viewed, first, as concerned with the
relation of each individual writer to the totality of expression,
it is concerned, secondly, with the relation of the totality of
writers to the totality of expression, and mediately, in the

third place, with the individual in relation to the totality of writers. Each style thus becomes reciprocally the differential of every other. To speak mathematically, the style of every writer represents some function of every other.

As a literature grows, it becomes obvious that the tendency of its writers in succession is to diverge from each other. But at a certain point it begins to be suspected that the mode of the new writers is in part a reproduction of the old. The principle of variation, in fact, is limited. Moreover, it tends to a limit, viz. the circumference of all variations, which is itself a new variety. And under that, either as a fact realised, or as a possibility, the separate orders of expression are seen to be vitally connected with each other, in so far as they are efficients of this common manifestation. The process is threefold. (1) The resultant varieties may be regarded independently, as antagonistic and complementary to each other. (2) From their limited number, and the common relationships existing among all, they tend to intersect and coincide with one another. (3) These tendencies are combined, so as to involve an antagonism to each, and a coincidence with all, in a variety which comprehends, and therefore supersedes all the rest. In this latter case, which is the most interesting and important, the relation of the writer is equally one of immanence and transcendence. This transcendence is not that which A exercises over B because he has so many more effects at his call; since B, in respect of that which is immanent in himself, transcends A. It is because the great writer is *not* transcended by any that he transcends all. And though his transcendence founds on the same basis as theirs, viz. immanence, that immanence is not of the ordinary type, the exclusive and *special* immanence of a distinctive range of expression absolutely his own. The ordinary immanence may be of two kinds, that which is common to all or that which is peculiar to each. In this case it is neither, but that which is peculiar to one in so far as it is distributed separately among all. Other writers of individuality, when the sum of all other individualities is taken, have something to add to it. To that sum he has nothing to add: it is identically his own distinction. If it is a sum of 25, in which A, B and C have each a share of one, it is clear that he transcends each by 24. Or if X happens to travel in the same way as himself, and musters up 13, him he transcends by 12; *i.e.* the gross result being taken, otherwise his superiority to X travels in a geometrical ratio. The ideal thus formed is no abstract ideal, but one that is essentially concrete, one in which all the elements are resolved. It is not meant, for example, that every peddling idiosyncrasy is included in the individuality of Shakspere. But those elements of expression are included like the wit of Ben Jonson, which are possessed by certain poets in special measure, and which go to integrate a totality of their own. And especially those pure and formal elements, which in some degree are possessed by all true poets, structural felicity and modulated intensity of expression—in simple terms, mastery of quantity and quality. How the catholic behaves when united with the individual, may be seen (in a dialectical shape) in relation to nationality. What we mean by a classic, is a writer who represents adequately the genius of his country, with sufficient force superadded of his own to expound that genius and make it interesting. It is only, therefore, by coalescing with a certain degree of force in

individuals, that the genius of a nation becomes a co-efficient
for its own illustration. It is quite another question to
what extent the appearance of such an individual may be
accidental, and whether it is the increase of the national
intelligence, or the increasing richness of national characteristic, that is the immediate occasion of that illustration.
I assume simply that the national bias will be found
directly represented in its literature, apart from this as a
possibility, that the very earliest literature was not preserved just because it was simple, and reflected no national
complexity of character, while only such legends were preserved as were connected *ex hypothesi* with the doings of
the race. But this very glorification of national tendencies
and national interests, defeats itself by demanding too
necessitously an increase of individual power. For obviously the supreme poet or the supreme thinker is not
national, but reflects the catholic in all nationality. But
his genius is not therefore anti-national. It is the danger
of a partial acuteness to conceive that a catholic genius is of
necessity opposed to a national. An English writer may,
in the first instance, by accident have the genius of a French-
man; in which case, of course, he *is* anti-national. Or,
secondly, he may have a truly catholic genius, in which
case his genius would infallibly be anti-national, but for the
chance of its coinciding, in the third place, with the
national genius, the nationality to which he belongs being
the most catholic. The common elements are glorified by
other nations in varying degrees, but by this in so perfect
a degree, as to become indefeasibly its differentia. The
catholic poets, the poets of intensity and compass, are those
of England; the catholic thinkers, the systematic thinkers,

are those of Germany. And, as notoriously Shakspere is
the unique catholic poet, so notoriously Hegel is the unique
catholic metaphysician. Absolutely catholic intellects they
are neither of them, since both are only partial; and absolutely catholic only that nation can be pronounced which
produces an intellect that shall be equally philosophic and
poetical. But evidently it is unjust, it is a perversion, to
exalt the individuality of either, as if it transcended the
national genius by its catholicity; when it is expressly as
being an outcome of that genius that it *is* catholic. Unjust
it is to the individual, since it represents his catholicity as
anti-national, which it is *not*, and to the nation, since it
represents as accidental what is essential.

Cor.—The function of a Logic is to give universals by
eliminating particulars. That which is common to all men
concretely in the midst of diversity, is the logical faculty;
that which is common to them, in spite of their common
logical faculty, is abstractly their diversity. Logic proper has
to deal with the first universal. And a Logic of Style is concerned with the second, a universal as complete and scientific
as the other; since every man has a differentia, as well as a
ground of community with other men. This universal is
Mode; a man's style being his mode, his manner, his
mannerism. The general questions concerned with this mode
are three. (1) As to the possible varieties of style which
may be possessed by any writer. In this respect he may
have a very complex differentiation; from the philosopher, for
example, he may be distinguished by being also a poet, and
vice versa; or from the poets and philosophers by some
special poetical or philosophic faculty; or, through the same
faculty, from those who like himself are both. (2) As to the

possible fluctuations in individual style within certain limits. Such may be produced by changes in health, by varying degrees of interest in the subject, or of aptitude for particular modes of expression, speaking and writing. (3) As to the coherence of his literary manner with his manner as a whole; how far that is controlled by his temperament, and consists with his personal habits and social bearing.

6.

The particular varieties of literary effect, with whatsoever complexity they may manifest themselves, rest notoriously upon a fundus of natural *sensibility*. This appears in three forms, (1) as creative, (2) as reproductive, and (3) as critical or negative.

That the same kind of power should be possessed by more than one man, does not make it less original, or what is meant specially by "genial." It is creative in so far as it is not communicable. And causing in the reader a desire to reproduce it, in the same breath it shows him his impotence to do anything but imitate it. For the distinction between reproduction and imitation is that the first obtains a revival of the principles of certain orders of effect, and the second merely a resemblance to certain isolated effects. And what imitation is ordinarily to reproduction, reproduction is in this case to creation; and accordingly, since *ex hypothesi* these effects are unique, any attempt to reproduce them falls to the level of imitation. For there are two orders of creative sensibility, which may be described as the faculty of developing the possibilities of expression. On the one hand it manifests itself as the power to devise new forms of

E

combination and simplification, etc., and on the other to
mature new orders of individual effect. It is, for example,
an approach to the expansion of style in the latter aspect,
to produce a peculiar mode of fanciful or humorous expression. And to the expansion of it in its former aspect,
it is a contribution, to discover a principle of transition by
which the general sense of elegance or economy is enhanced, at the same time that the demands of the case for
fulness are adequately met. The former element *tends*
sometimes in the direction of eccentricity ; which is in any
case revolting, because it is either unaffected, in which case
it is monstrous, or assumed, in which case it is insolent.
But the eccentricity, which immediately I speak of, arises
just from attempting externally to reproduce what is
absolutely original in another man's expression, and so falling into grotesque travestie. And the tendency is the more
dangerous, because the result is for many people so much
more striking than quieter and more perfect effects. Hence
its essential vulgarity, which consists, not in preferring
what is loud to what is unobtrusive, but in preferring what
is simply clumsy to what is forcible. For there is a sphere
in which higher effects are attainable, and with the
additional privilege of being legitimate, and not essentially
futile. This is the alternative sphere indicated, in which
the copyists may be as successful as the original artists,
provided they have the power readily to appropriate the
turns of thought devised by earlier writers, and to employ
them in their variety and relevance. To a certain extent,
therefore, this power is accompanied by a power that is
critical or negative. Generally, it manifests itself in
perceiving that certain turns of expression are in them-

selves vulgar and clumsy, and for ever, therefore, irrelevant. In its higher form, it consists of a discrimination of effects, which in themselves are valid, as invalid in certain relations —inadequate, redundant, or vicious. For not the perception merely or chiefly of what is good in itself is the test of true sensitiveness, but of what is good in certain circumstances. Such a sensibility will manifest itself, therefore, in the repudiation of every mode of expression that is incongruous with the prevailing cast of thought, or the general structure of a proposition; in the perception, that this or that expression requires to be expunged or modified, as affecting too severe a qualification of a certain idea, or requires modification before it can operate adequately as an exponent of the spirit of a certain passage. Most obviously, this capacity is useful in critically reorganising and re-modelling one's own compositions. Every writer feels the necessity more or less of altering his first draught of a composition for the better, not only in the conception and *motif*, and the modification of long reaches of thinking, by the resources of transposition, and the altering of distant proportions, or the interpolation of new ideas, etc., but in the diction itself.

COR.—What is good in an author's expression may be rather the reflex of good thinking otherwise, than the result of a general capacity for Style. The more logically, for instance, a man thinks, the less will he be disposed to write with any *extra* measure of gracefulness. Yet that of itself is a guar-antee for a certain quality of elegance. And where he is most of all in a condition to benefit by his logic, is where it coexists with the independent facilities and graces of expres-sion. There is, in fact, no collateral agency, whether of

intellect or of temper, that may not co-operate to individual
force of style. And no writer is above being improved by
the aid of the machinery which exists internally for ratify-
ing his distinctive brilliance as an artist, in the way of reproduction and revision. Naturally, in connection with revision,
it sounds paradoxical to say that a man is inevitably an artist,
whose original execution leaves much to remodel, and no artist,
because it leaves nothing to amend. For evidently it is just
the impracticable blockhead, who will find it most difficult
to vary his original conceptions. In this, however, he is
formally on a level with the greatest of impromptu performers.
And what is intended is, that, with every necessity for
amendment, there must exist a corresponding ability to meet
it. In the case of the blockhead, the necessity for improvement exists at a maximum, with the minimum power of
counteraction; with the supreme artist it exists at a minimum, with the additional pleasant condition of a critical taste
at its maximum. Certainly a happy adjustment applied to
continuous expression is a crucial test of the artist, under conditions of success so liable to disturbance, even from physical
causes. And if in such circumstances the mental balance is
disturbed, it is evident to what extent it must draw upon its
facilities for repeal and amendment. Apart from this, the
critical faculty is constantly used in the original composition.
And that it is not needed for subsequent correction is due,
not to the spontaneity of the mind in that original effort
having overridden the necessity for it, but precisely to its
having itself been in full play; that it is required ultimately,
being a sign *pro tanto* of its not having co-operated originally
to produce a satisfactory result.

Section III.   Of Style in its relation in Rhetoric.

7.

The method of Style is essentially that of a *Critique, i.e.* a separation or dis-cernment of individual expressions from each other, in so far as it has to do with expression, and of individual complements of expression from each other, in so far as it has to do with individuals. This method, on the one side, is distinguished from the dialectical, by placing its specific results and items as ultimate and permanent, and expressly as not having a tendency to pass into each other. On the other, the science is distinguished from Rhetoric, whose function it is to apply the data of expression; and which stands, therefore, as the practical science of Style.

A man's literary power is *pro tanto* a fund of expression; indestructible, but capable of being modified within certain limits, of being extended or intensified, limited or suppressed. The final question, in the case where one writer is pitted against another, is as to the adaptation of their respective styles to the circumstances. And thus expressions begin to acquire invidiously, so to speak, and by way of rivalry, a certain value as opposed to each other. The duty of every artist is accordingly, (1) to develop his own special skill of diction, (2) to supplement it with whatever he may lawfully reproduce from the common fund of expression, and (3) to adapt the several varieties of diction to the separate circumstances in which he thinks accommodation is demanded—which may include expressly the abnegation of the more luxurious or even more catholic affects for the sake of the lower and coarser. The science of

this distribution, affiliating itself to Style at this point, is
Rhetoric; and its function on the negative side is to con-
travene and truncate mere stylic brilliance, where that is
necessary—to reproduce spontaneity in chasteness of proportion, and the transcendental in the practical, and, generally,
to insist on the subordination of immediate to mediate
effect. Thus high literary effort upon a magnificent scale
is a desirable thing in relation to the literary ideal. But
the high style on occasion may be useless, and for effect
virtually lower than one absolutely less forcible. That
collision, however, may be resolved, and the former ideal
restored, if it should happen that *culture* could be given,
by not condescending to the immediate exigencies. There
are degrees of merit in the different standards. Nor does
the higher artist supersede the lower, even if *his* literary
culture be merely secondary, and superinduced by the
necessity to write, because some men must read him—*i.e.*
are compelled to apply to him for instruction—who have
no occasion to study the higher models. Even *he*, the
journeyman author, the conscript, has it in his power to
raise the art as an art, (1) by raising the average standard
of execution, (2) the standard of appreciation, (3) the professional standard, stimulated by the non-professional
sympathy, and reacting upon it.

Cor.—This distinction is the broad external distinction
between Rhetoric and Style, according to which the one is the
regulative science of the facts which *constitute* the other. The
condition of *origin* being satisfied, in Style, Rhetoric deals with
the conditions of *result*. A man is bound, in the first instance,
by individual, local, or professional bias; his individuality
combating these elements perhaps, or coalescing with them to

a good or a bad purpose. These he may wish, in the next
instance, to foster or to overcome for certain ends. And so
there arises the teleologic ideal, according to which it is determined not what the man ought absolutely to be, but what he
ought relatively to be.

8.

Style is distinguished more especially from Rhetoric, by
taking account of ideas immediately connected with each
other in detail, while Rhetoric is the science of passages and
pieces in their totality. To regard an entire paragraph, as
offering a relief to another, for example, is rhetorical and para-
stylic. The two sciences become thus complementary modes
of viewing any particular passage. For it may quite easily
happen that the individual expressions are good, but that the
disposition of the larger masses is confused or disproportionate,
or that the total conception is clear, but the diction clumsy,
etc., there being thus not one criterion, but two criteria. The
distinction is most easily illustrated from a complete piece,
and one whose outlines are few even if complex, as for example
a poem, which allows a special condensation :—

BIRTH AND DEATH.[1]

Ever gaze to each other two figures, one lit with the light
Of earth's sunshine, and one in the shadow thrown back from the
    bright
Larger sun of the future. Lo, Birth, but a child : her bright hair,
That life's breeze gently stirs on her forehead so snowily fair,
Ripples golden and glad in the sunlight, and mirth's frolic beam
In her eyes' azure dances, unwitting of that sombre dream

From " First Fruits and Shed Leaves:" by the Author of "The Wreck of
    the Northfleet."

That darkens the distance.   *Joy-parted, her mouth seems to sip*
With cleft coral the exuberant brightness that breaks on her lip.
As frail-seeming and white as a mist-wreath, her garment o'erclings
Her flesh softly moulded and rosy as when the light springs
With last kiss from the ardorous sunset to cloud in the east—
So pure are her young limbs and rosy, so dimpled and creased.

As silent and dark as a shadow, unmoved as a stone
That standeth all day in the desert, unseen and alone,
Waiteth Death : no breeze touches her *mantle that falleth right*
    down
Over feet that we see not and hands that we see not; a frown
Seems to drift down the distance and blight the fresh pastures of
    life,
And an icy breath seems to blow from her and make the air rife
With tremblings.   And yet as we gaze in her fathomless eyes
The charm of her beauty awakens, although her hair lies
White and thinly laid over her forehead's mysterious shade
(That looms with a beauty no earth-light may ever invade),
And her fine lips together are set in a sadness divine,
Too deep and too holy for sorrow—each loveliest line
Of her limbs 'neath her raiment of shadow a presence becomes,
And a scent broodeth round her far sweeter than odours of spices
    or gums.

This poem in its totality is essentially subtle.   There is,
first, a broad and obvious antithesis between Birth and Death
—Birth in her morning beauty, and Death in her austere
repellance.   But secondly, a contrast is introduced between
Death in this aspect, and Death in a more auspicious aspect,
as being spiritually its own euthanasy, and the emancipator
of the soul into life.   But is this all ?   Not, certainly, according to the genial significance of the poem.   For in the third
instance, there is the contrast between Death, no longer Death
the sullen, but Death the serene, and the unchanged joyous-
ness of Birth.   And here is what *might* be the coincidence of

Death and Birth. Negate Birth, and you have Death; negate Death, and you have Birth. That is, in the ordinary dialectic. But the special subtlety of this conception is not merely, having differentiated Death from Birth, to differentiate it again from itself, but to differentiate it so that, under the last aspect, it shall still be differentiated from Birth, and not repeat any of the characteristic imagery *there*. The dialectic is the true dialectic, by which *both* elements are held resolved in a higher medium. Such is the *motif*, or rhetorical aspect of the poem. Now obviously enough, the imagery which runs in a series of parallels expounding the general conception, reflects in detail the dominant idea of the piece. But, apart from that, it has a purely stylic value, according to the degree of beauty and precision with which it expresses the separate idea that it is intended to convey. Thus, independently, the italicised passages are perfect in their effect. The one expresses the redundancy of delicate sensuousness—delicate, because sipping just catches the aspect of the lingeringly parted lip, redundant, because the lip is painted as tasting, *i.e. receiving*, a radiance, of which its own redness is in part the cause, *i.e. diffuses*. The other expresses the sense of mystery, in the veiling of the feet and hands, since the hand and the foot are just the members that universally in ordinary use, and for the sake of freedom of touch and movement, are left uncovered by the mantle.

It happens that, mediately, through their relation to the common totality, individual expressions have a relation to each other, which are not immediately connected. Stylic connection of individual propositions is with those which stand next to them in the process of thinking; rhetorical connection of separate thoughts is that in which they recip-

rocally illuminate each other at remoter distances. A piece
like " Birth and Death," so rich in felicitous concurrences,
and so frugal in its anxiety not to expend a single unneces-
sary thought or image, abounds in this kind of complementary significance. The beauty of Death has been
demonstrated not merely to comprehend the beauty of
Birth, but to transcend it. And that is the significance of
" *a scent* broodeth round her," &c., as opposed rhetorically
to the mere phase of vision in Birth. This reservation
marks a severely intellectual style of treatment. For the
sensuousness in the representation of Birth had reached, it
might have been supposed, a limit. And yet beyond that
limit, upon the necessity arising, the luxuriance is pressed,
the scent expressing a redundance of luxury that the mere
sight could never give. A subtler sense is brought into
action, and, as it happens, a rarer sensory even within that,
for the effect is not deadened by a description of the scent,
which simply is *not* that " of spices or gums "—an essence
that no flame of earth may ever kindle, and that æons of
ritual will not burn away. The significance of this part is
enhanced by its position as the concluding idea of the piece.
For by drafting the imagery into a separate world of sense,
the movement of the poem, towards its climax, is translated
suddenly into a transcendent region, and locked up into a
perpetual rest, inviolate as cathedrals, and of cathedral
stillness.

COR.—Apart from the indirect significance every individual
expression ought to have in relation to the piece of which it
forms a part, and from the significance it may reflect upon
other individual expressions, it may occasionally have a direct
rhetorical significance. Why, in the concluding phase of this

poem, should death be represented as sad with "a sadness divine, too deep and too holy for sorrow," when it is felt that (according to the Christian conception) she is the medium of immortality? Obviously enough, the association of jubilance being preoccupied by Birth, if the totality of the conception is to be integrated, a contrast must be preserved between the two. Yet that is quite beside the point. Even literary symmetry must vanish, must be abolished, unless it coincides with the radical truth on the question. It is also evident, but not more pertinent, that if Death were represented as jubilant, in a moment would go to ruin the primary conception of her as sullen. And as a matter of fact in the execution, this cohesion of the character is beautifully preserved against contradiction in the contrasted phases late and early—to match the melancholy sweetness of the one there is no scowl, but a frown, nor even a frown, but what "seems" to be a frown. That primary conception, nevertheless, gives the cue to the representation of Death, and is determined, antecedently to all artistic considerations, by the natural feeling which it betokens, that of instinctive awe. For here the poem is entirely subjective: her dreadful aspect representing our feeling of dread. And hence in the sequel her sorrow for us means our sorrow, our anxiety for ourselves; her attitude being one in spirit with our own; neither maliciously jubilant over her power of destruction, nor gratuitously jubilant over the reversionary gain; too "holy" for the one, too "deep" for the other. Nor is that any marvel, seeing that the mood of Death is too "deep" and too "holy" for sorrow; a fortiori, therefore, as regards rejoicing. Yet that which is too profound and too spiritual for vulgar grief, as it is for vulgar jubilation, is not joy, but sadness; and necessarily so, in accordance with the subjective feeling. But

why "deep," and why " holy " ? Because, in the one case, it is
associated with reflection, in the other, because it is unselfish.
And the grief of sadness is infinitely deeper than the grief of
sorrow, because expounded by a power of reflection, by which
Death sees herself as a universal agency, remembering all
whom she has destroyed, and thinking of all those whom she
must destroy; and infinitely holier, because she grieves not
for herself the inevitable destroyer, but for us whom she
destroys. That is the philosophic rendering of the truth of
the distinction, and that is also the stylic significance of the
expression. What now of its rhetorical application to the
whole final conception of Death as sad ? It founds upon the
essential *passivity*, expressed in the words " deep" and " holy."
Death knows no casual victims, and grieves with no petulant
grief, since she is no arbitrary instrument, but the fulfilling of
a fatality, which being necessary must for that very reason be
just, and not to be made the occasion of sickly grief,—and
being just, must be laden with some reversionary hope. Still
that hope, being yet in reversion, is not to be saluted with
boisterous anticipation. The figure of Death is still turned
toward us, as an experience that must be faced; though its
illumination is from beyond. But since its significance, if
understood in its intense passivity, is not more that of a universal than that of a mediate necessity, the *indirect* suggestion
of the one by the other is infinitely more subtle and pregnant,
than if the figure had been turned round amid the blare of
anthems and the blaze of resurrection.

9.

Besides the indirect significance which any passage may bear,
there is for every passage an indirect literary effect, superadded

to its immediate stylic effect. This superadded effect is also rhetorical, as contradistinguished from the stylic.

The two canons according to which literary effect is most rapidly determined are these two—force and artistic beauty. There is no effective passage, of which we cannot say it is either forcible or beautiful. But obviously every passage that is forcible is also to a certain extent beautiful, and *vice versa.* That a man does not generally admire the way in which he has been knocked down, does not disprove this; his irritation may interfere to prevent it. But that in a single instance he has so far abstracted from his personal feeling as to admire a telling blow of that kind, is a complete proof that the exhibition of modulated power has of itself a reflex æsthetic value. So also the mere view of a fragile object, a petal, or a piece of porcelain, conveys *pro tanto* a sense of power. Even verbally they may be shown to have a certain identity. By " effect," in common phrase, we mean, on the one hand, palpable result; and a thing is effective just in proportion as it produces such a result. But a thing done " for effect," on the other hand, expresses the last definite purpose assignable for any exertion whatever—the sublation of all ordinary purpose—viz. an æsthetic purpose. The phrase has become partly one of contempt. But it is legitimate, seeing that the æsthetic purpose is itself a teleologic purpose, and the teleologic value in that case is exactly proportioned to the æsthetic result. It is the same with literary effect :—

How sweet is thy love, O my sister, my betrothed !
How sweet is thy love above wine !
And the fragrance of thy perfumes above all the spices !
Thy lips, O my betrothed, distil honey ;
Honey and milk are under thy tongue,

And the odour of thy garments is as the smell of Lebanon.
A closed garden art thou, my sister, my betrothed,
A closed garden, a sealed fountain.
Thy shoots like a garden of pomegranates,
With precious fruits,
Cypresses and nards,
Nard and crocus,
Calamus and cinnamon,
With all sorts of frankincense trees,
Myrrh and aloes ;
With all kinds of excellent aromatics,
With a garden-fountain,
A well of living waters,
And streams flowing from Lebanon.
Arise, O north wind ! and come, thou south !
Blow upon my garden,
That its perfumes may flow out !

There is no immediate force of expression here ; nevertheless it produces for us not merely a sense of power in the artist, but a sense of force that is not in spite of, but directly proportioned to, the beauty in the expression. And so conversely :—

The mouth is amply developed. Brutalities unspeakable sit upon the upper lip, which is confinent with a snout ; for separate nostrils there are none. But the lower lip, which is drawn inwards with the curve of a marine shell—oh, what a convolute of cruelty and revenge is there ! Cruelty !—to whom ? Revenge !—for what ? Pause not to ask ; but look upwards to other mysteries. In the very region of his temples, driving itself downwards into his cruel brain, and breaking the continuity of his diadem, is a horrid chasm, a ravine, a shaft, that many centuries would not traverse ; and it is serrated on its posterior wall with a harrow that is partly hidden. From the anterior wall of this chasm rise, in vertical directions, two processes ; one perpendicular, and rigid as a horn, the other streaming forward before some portentous breath.[1]

[1] *Description of the Nebula in Orion :* by De Quincey.

Not an image of beauty is here; yet extrinsically, and because of its essential force, a reflex æsthetic sense is produced. And but for its force this effect would not be given. Directly it excludes beauty just as much as weakness. But that which in itself excludes beauty becomes thus the mediator of it in relation to expressions which seemed calculated to express the reverse, viz. repulsiveness. The indirect effect in both these cases is rhetorical, that is to say, it is not distinctively the same for either, but alternatively. It may be difficult at times to say which is the immediate effect, and which the derived, since they meet in every passage. But the same causes which operate to make the relation dual, and, therefore, on occasion, equivocal, necessarily operate as a ground for distinguishing which is the derived, and which the immediate, whether beauty or force.

COR.—The rhetorical principle holds true in the converse case, that whatever is generally inartistic is to that extent weak, and whatever is weak is inartistic. But whether negatively, or positively, the rhetorical possibilities of effect, as well as those of stylic effect on which they found, rest ultimately on the possibilities of the formation and aggregation, the differentiating and the grouping of individual expressions, in their simple ultimate relations of Quality and Quantity. Of these the primary relation is that of Quality.

CHAPTER II.

OF QUALITY.

Section I. The Conditions of Quality.

10.

THE universal criterion for style, first and last, is effect. If a man calls you a fool, he produces a result, because of some issue or principle suggested, and connecting itself with some sentiment—of chagrin or astonishment, of pain or resentment, etc. Now the inevitable co-factor in all such cases is novelty. The proposition advanced need not be substantially new; it may be identically a repetition of an old charge or statement. But that mere quantitative or numerical difference is sufficient to create a sensation of novelty. It is not that you have not been told so before; but it is that you are now told so by a different person. Or perhaps it is not even that; but it is that you are now told it by the same person a second time. That of itself stimulates the attention, apart from the stimulus otherwise lent by the fact that something was to be said, which you expected to be something new. And the faculties of reproduction are known implicitly to be so weak, that your informant trusts either to your having forgotten it, or else you politely bear with it, trusting that he has forgotten having said it. And if not, you revolt. You did not come there, you say, to learn that, or you did not pay to hear that, etc.

And supposing what you are told to be something like this, that six and five make eleven, you rebel, because an effect is produced which you cannot get rid of, and which is produced, just because the statement which occasions it is not novel. That being your desideratum, perhaps even your *sine qua non*, the result is not immediately, because the statement is commonplace, but mediately, because it is not original.

In so far as logic is the immediate science of truth, it supplies any essential virtue that might be found to belong to an art like style in expounding truth. What style receives for itself is only a certain percentage of commission for making the truth tell. The amount of its profits, however, is determined, not merely by the degree of its success, but by the amount of truth which it communicates. This is the second and implicit condition of style, just as logic, after its own fashion, acknowledges the condition of originality. There is no need, it is felt there, of illustrating the multiplication-table; all that must be left to the illuminator, or embosser on new patterns. And even in testing a proposition accepted as true, the tester is virtually assuming that it is not known to be true. When attested, therefore, it is *pro tanto* original; truth becoming thus a synthetic idea. And conversely, originality, instead of meaning simply that which is not known, comes to mean that which is not known to be true.

COR.—The absolute criterion of all suggestion is truth; novelty is only relative. But, as it happens, style deals distinctively with the relative, leaving logic to deal with the absolute. It is to be distinctly observed, however, that the relativity of truth ascribed to style *is* that of novelty, not of particularity. A statement, according to literary modes of dealing,

7

is relatively true for a man for whom it was not true before,
not as being true for him, because false for some one else.
The purpose of style is not simply to defend or aggrandise a
foregone conclusion in any man's mind, dividing the world on
any particular question into two factions, those who believe
the one phase, and those who believe the other.   The division
which it makes is of all men into two sections, those who
know a truth, and those who know it not (a much more universal division than the other, since that upon most questions
leaves a third space open and indifferent), or, it may be, those
who know it adequately, and those who know it inadequately.
For as soon as a truth is announced, and to some extent
recognised, there is a call to intensify the impression at the
moment, and make the truth better known—known more
clearly, more forcibly, more captivatingly.   If the idea is apprehended as yet only in figure, explicate it literally ; if it is
scientifically obscure, bring it through figure into a clearer
apprehension.   Have the data become stale ?—let them be
vivified by historical illustration ; or superannuated ?—let
them be supplemented by later researches, so as to equate the
interest of the listener, on the one hand, with their importance,
and on the other, with their fertility.   The result in this case is
not, as in the first, where the gain to one side is a dead loss to
the other, but always a positive advantage ; and, for the
individual, of knowledge experimental instead of visionary,
and of knowledge coherent instead of confused and partial.

11.

All effect, depending ultimately on the conditions of novelty
and truth, is produced mediately through the terms of separate
propositions, through the mutual relations of subject and pre-

dicata. This is what constitutes Quality in style generally ; in which *it is identical as to its basis with Quantity in logic.*

The quality of a thought is that which makes it to differ from other thoughts, to be that which distinctively it is. In logic, all this descends upon the copula ; and the differentiation there is of the simplest ; for no matter in what way the subject and predicate behave, the question revolves upon us : Is it, or is it not so ? With a different criterion, the differentiation of style is more complex ; it allows of various kinds and degrees of effect, where logic allows of none. And hence the fact that the onus of the differentiation settles upon the subject and predicate. In logic, novelty being satisfied (*i.e.* postulated), the question of truth devolves upon the copula. Which implicit canon of observance being settled for style, the explicit stylic condition is fulfilled in the subject and predicate. It would be spurious to insist upon the distinction between truth and novelty, as if the first were related specially to the subject, and the latter to the predicate. It is to a certain extent true, that, since the predicate comes last, the attention apprehends the novelty of the conception, only when the final term is distinctly rapped out, and its truth, only when it travels back upon the subject, to compare the one with the other. In fact neither term acts without the other. And as logic claims the copula, *in* which its results are determined, *through* the subject and predicate, so style lays claim to the latter, *in* which its results are determined *through* the copula. And this happens not in spite of, but because of the fact, that the terms and the copula are capable of reciprocal variation (by permutation, etc.). Also it happens not in spite of, but expressly because of the fact,

that each science is governed fundamentally by the same
laws.

COR.—Quality in the scientific sense is obviously to be discriminated from any thoughtless figurative use of the term
applied to what are certain *properties* of style (loosely called
qualities) or quasi-rhetorical criteria (§ 9, p. 77), founding
upon this one elementary and homogeneous fact of quality.
It would evidently be a very coarse and a very gratuitous
confusion, to place such properties of style as Force and
Beauty in the same category with the *elements* of style, such,
for example, as sublimity. (1.) These properties form a distinct set of criteria, applicable to any passage, superadded to
the criteria which determine its effect as regulated by the
amount of sentiment. And to place both under a common
category is, therefore, the same thing as to classify together
wool, platinum, hardness and flexibility. Metaphor and
other elements are quite overlooked in this process, which have
equal right to go into the category of so-called qualities
with sublimity. And the gist of their exclusion is, that as
elements they are left to be qualified by the properties including sublimity; which means precisely that tin and copper,
etc., are qualified in respect of certain attributes, such as hardness, flexibility—and iron! (2.) While the properties of style
involve each other reciprocally (§ 9), the elements of style do
not; they are either indifferent, as in metaphor and sublimity,
or else mutually exclusive, as in sublimity and humour. (3.)
The properties of style are to be found in *every* thought; the
elements are only occasional, *i.e.* variable merely and alternative. *Every* thought is more or less clear, more or less beautiful, more or less forcible; the properties come directly into
question in regard to every expression, and in their totality.

Some element of expression must, of course, be in every thought, but each, as it were, only in rotation.

12.

The principle by which a term is divided, according as it signifies certain attributes, or the number of objects to which these may be extended, is known under some name or other to all readers. It might be supposed that for style, if any change of nomenclature were required, it would be sufficient to introduce some phrase which might express the essentially compound nature of the connotation in its terms. That, in fact, is not the case, but the reverse; since the very relation which calls attention to the connotation of attributes in a compound, calls attention to the fact that each complex term is divisible into attributes numerically separate. Accordingly, by the *inclusion* of a term is meant, in relation to style, the aggregation of a certain number of attributes, and by its *implication*, its comprehension of a certain congeries of individuals. The implication of "thing," for example, is universal; since it covers all objects indifferently, and, without a hint of the brilliance and mass of whatsoever attributes they may include, itself most meagre in respect of that inclusion which it vilipends in other terms. This is borne out in a somewhat paradoxical way. When a boarding-school young lady does not dare to be directly and maliciously impudent, or is too excited or too refined to express herself with vehemence, she calls her friend and enemy a "thing;" where the very absence of all positive inclusion is the ground of the derived significance. The individual is denuded of all that constitutes individuality in the sense affecting her—is reduced to the individuality which distinguishes one farthing from another. And the term is applied with most effect to a person, since from a person there is most to take away. This is the opposite case, viz., depth of inclusion. For, agreeably to the dual meaning of the term, individuality, which, on the one side, signifies abstract identity, an identity which one other individual is sufficient to expound, signifies also a concrete identity, which it may take an infinite variety of others to expound.

The more common and superficial relations of description and distribution (as opposed to definition and division) are essentially stylio in their adaptation. Description, for example, by way of simile—*e.g.* a stammerer being described, as one who had swallowed the alphabet without chewing it, and in revenge had to go through the process of mastication when needing to use it—is highly in the manner of style. To call a man "both knave and fool" is quite allowable, as a matter of description. But a very comical mode of description is to counterfeit the technical machinery of division, as in saying that a man is "*half* knave and half fool," the man being indivisible in that sense, and indescribable, therefore, if he were so divided.

COR.—Quality as such in style has a definite meaning, in so far as it is to be distinguished from a possible quantity; and a technical meaning, in so far as it is to be contradistinguished from logical quality. A second meaning which may be attached to it is the metaphysical. And accordingly, I draw attention, for the moment, to the fact of the internal relations of propositions generally, thus :—

Quantity.	*Quality.*		*Mode.*
All	Men	(are)	Hypocrites.

Thirdly, however, it happens that, in common phrase, the

relations, which here are seen to commingle, may be spoken
of as convertible with each other. Accordingly, if I proclaim
the fact that all men are hypocrites, I shall receive the next
day anonymous letters, requesting, indifferently as regards the
expression (though peremptorily enough, in all likelihood, as
regards the intention), that the statement shall be " qualified,"
or " modified." " Quantified," as being a trifle too scientific
and, therefore, too calm for an anonymous letter, would not
be used. Nevertheless, either of the three terms may be
applied to any of the specific functions of the proposition.
And as " modify," which means first of all to accentuate, or be
the cause of the accentuation of any specific difference in
an object, comes to signify a *variation* of the present state
of the object, so " quantify" comes to signify a variation in
the numerical relations or possibilities of any term. The predicate, therefore, which strictly is modal, may also be quantified. Only it is a variation of its *inclusion* which takes place,
not of its implication; the distinction of the altered term
being, not that it is specifically connected with this or that
subject, to the exclusion of other subjects, but that it is connected with this or that subject to the exclusion of other predicates. Its value is determined accordingly either by way of
its being preferred to other predicates generally, or differentially, by way of its being preferred to such as from their
resistance are hard to supersede. That being understood, it
does not matter how I amend my statement, whether by
quantifying, qualifying, or modifying. Only that most appropriately (according to the scheme already given), when I am
asked to retract my paradox, I quantify it, by saying " *some*
men are hypocrites;" being pressed still farther, I qualify it,
by saying "some *wicked* men are hypocrites," and finally,

being pressed into something like the truth, modify it, by
acknowledging in desperation, that "some wicked men are
occasionally hypocrites." With regard to which it may be
noticed (1) that the critical term in every proposition is the
middle term, the qualitative, which preserves an equivocal
relation to the others, changing what is ushered into it from
quantity in the shape of implication, into the shape of inclusion when that is transferred to mode. (2) The ratios of
variation are the same, both for implication and inclusion, in
so far as both vary numerically. Thus an "all" is always
greater than a "some." (3) The subject and predicate expound and modify each other, and that directly, through the
common relations of implication and inclusion. A diminution
of the implication of the subject is followed by an expansion
of the inclusion of the predicate, and conversely. Also a
diminution of the implication or inclusion of the subject is
accompanied by a corresponding diminution in the implication
or inclusion of the predicate; and similarly in regard to its
expansion. But while the process of variation may be expounded numerically, the immediate ground of the variation
is essentially one of quality. The union of two attributes is
not simply one of numerical increment, but one of combination. "Quaint," for example, which, abstractly considered, is
the synthesis of *two* conceptions, to wit peculiarity, with an
element of simplicity, is really qualitative, in so far as one of
these attributes, at least, is complex, and itself *a fortiori* is a
unity of complex meaning. The general principles, according
to which the variation of quality is determined, are Subtlety
and Comprehensiveness.

Section II. Of Subtlety.

13.

Every truth that is determined negatively, *i.e.* by way of resistance to, or essential variation upon some antecedent conception, falls, like every truth that is simply positive, under one of three categories : it is either an All, a Some, or a None. And it does so, by way of contradistinction to some one of the correlative formulæ. The disaffection is organic ; each form being complementary to the rest, not simply as a positive resource for meeting a specific emergency, but negatively, as an exponent of the value and significance of the form against which for the time being it is measured. Accordingly the form of every proposition may be explicated thus, the thesis representing the fallacious version, and the antithesis the amended version :—

Thesis.			Antithesis.
No	P is Q.	(*Univ.*)	All P is Q.
No	P is Q.	(*Part.*)	Some P is Q.
All	P is Q.	(*Sing.*)	Some P is Q.

and conversely :—

Thesis.			Antithesis.
All	P is Q.	(*Univ.*)	No P is Q.
Some	P is Q.	(*Part.*)	No P is Q.
Some	P is Q.	(*Sing.*)	All P is Q.

The implication of the terms is thus expanded, in the first section of the scheme, and restricted in the second. Accordingly, a *restrictive universal* is formed by reducing an all to a none, and an *expansive universal*, by extending a none to an all ; and the particular is restricted and expanded correspondingly. In the case of singular propositions, however, the reverse takes place. To reduce an all to a some is to expand the force of what is thus restricted, and to raise the appreciable value of the term as singular—as sole and peculiar. And so to reduce the force of a singular proposition is not to reduce it to a blank negation, but to make it indistinguishable and general, by expanding the some to an all. Any fallacy *there* consists in equating all P with Q, when what should have been equated with Q was simply some portion or function of P, viz. p. But now, let P be measured against other terms, as being itself the singular equivalent for the predicate Q; and the fallacy will consist in equating the generic term, say S, with Q, to the obscuring of P. P is here a portion of S; and, by substituting S for P, you neutralise the specific value of P. But by substituting S, you have altered the *inclusion* of the term: so long as the talk was of P simply, there was only change of implication; but now that you have brought in S, and expanded the implication (from $P =$ some S, to all S) you have restricted the inclusion. Hitherto, I had held that only those refined-men-who-were-easily-provoked were backbiters, but you disabuse me of that belief, by insisting that all refined men, more or less, are backbiters. But now, upon this suggestion of a variation in the inclusion of a term, follows another change. You tell me, for example, that "all language is progressive, save in very rude and early periods," and I am startled by the proposition, having been accustomed to regard language as then most aggressive, when much remained to be discovered in the way of new ideas, and most stationary, when literature had developed, and made men everywhere conversant with the whole complement of ideas. But the form, under which the new conception presents itself to me is this, surprise that *anything* in language should be associated with progression—in the technical for-

mula, that any P should be Q. By and by, I may realise the
fact, that all language is progressive, by pitting that proposition (all P is Q) against the other (some P is Q), and so,
mediately, pitting it against the original one, no P is Q. The
distinction, in regard to this form of proposition, is that it
eliminates the negative universal of the first schema, and
substitutes, under a different valuation, what was the singular
form as its particular, having provided itself with a new
singular, determined, not internally and by preserving the
same term (P), but externally, and by repudiating a new
generic form, S, thus :—

Thesis.		*Antithesis.*
Some P is Q.	(*Univ.*)	All P is Q.
No P is Q.	(*Part.*)	Some P is Q.
All S is Q.	(*Sing.*)	Only P is Q.

and negatively:—

Thesis.		*Antithesis.*
All P is Q.	(*Univ.*)	Some P is Q.
Some P is Q.	(*Part.*)	No P is Q.
Only P is Q.	(*Sing.*)	All S is Q.

Evidently, therefore, in the positive part of the schema, the
universal antithesis is formed upon the thesis, by expanding the
implication, the particular, by expanding the inclusion, and
the singular, by restricting the implication. And in the
privative section, the universal antithesis is formed, by
restricting the implication, the particular, by restricting the
inclusion, and the singular, by expanding the implication.

Now subtlety, in general, consists precisely (with the help of
surprise) in the legitimate variation of one or other of these
formulæ to its antithetic formula; and always by means of
the *inclusion* of the proposition. For any variation in a proposition, whether real or fancied, depends upon some variation, real or spurious, in its inclusion. Its terms need not

vary verbally; but they must substantially, so that the variation shall be reciprocally expounded by each. If a man tells me that the dogma of Papal Infallibility is a regulative and practical, as opposed to a constitutive and essential doctrine, he expands for me the permanent inclusion of the dogma, on that side at least. But, at the same moment, he has added to the implication of the term "regulative," as extended to this very dogma. Accordingly, in this instance, in which it is the inclusion of the subject that is expanded, the variation is advertised by a corresponding expansion in the implication of the predicate. Here, however, appears what might be a blank contradiction to the principle of variation (as expressed on p. 88), affecting the inverse movement of expansion and implication in subject and predicate. The rationale, nevertheless, is clear: "any" and "none" cannot be measured the one against the other, as if they stood to each other as genus and species, or *vice versa*; they are contraries, and not partial coincidents. But the moment it is a question of reciprocal variation of terms, where they may be compared as genus to species, or species to genus, the principle of inversion takes effect; as in fact it does here with regard to the other forms of variation in propositions. The subject and predicate vary reciprocally thus (the particular proposition being here made to usurp the position of the universal) in the positive scheme :—

The Particular (some P, as against no P) expands the inclusion of the subject, and the implication of the predicate.

The Universal (all P, as against some P) restricts the inclusion of the subject, and expands the implication of the predicate.

The Singular (only P, as against all S) expands the inclusion of the subject, and restricts the implication of the predicate.

In the negative:—

The Particular (no P, as against some P) restricts the inclusion of the subject, and the implication of the predicate.

The Universal (some P, as against all P) expands the inclusion of the subject, and restricts the implication of the predicate.

The Singular (all S, as against P simply) restricts the inclusion of the subject, and expands the implication of the predicate.

So far, however, there is nothing to discriminate what is subtle from what is novel. You tell us that your brother has joined a secret society. The terms certainly expound each other; but there is no subtlety in your statement, and if there could be, it would be in the fact, not in *you*. And were it not that the subtlety would be in *us*, for suggesting it, we should advise you to go and look your brother well round, and see if he is not immensely corpulent, and then come and tell us that he had gained admission to the society through the keyhole. For in some such fashion must you strike the manner of subtlety, *i.e.* in a proposition, whose terms do not appear immediately to reciprocate, as to their *differential* restriction and expansion. It will astonish people to hear that corpulence should include anything like getting through a keyhole, and that getting through a keyhole should implicate anything in the shape of corpulence.

Any variation of a truth that is logically coherent must itself be definite. Only, in logic, it is quite enough, if the alteration rests with the antithesis, and simply says that the thesis is *not* what it was asserted to be. But this is not sufficient, according to style. There it is indispensable to assign the counter-position, to say *what* a thing is or is not, and *how much* of it. And thus it happens, that many a writer, bent simply on the exposition of his subject, and concerning himself not in the least about his logic, or about the possible objections he may be meeting, is reversing whole trains of thought in the minds of his readers, without being aware that he is overriding theories of which he has never heard, and without even being reminded that he is colliding with theories which he knows very well. It is a commonplace fact, that a man may write well, and may reason well, without knowing how he does it. But the real point of such a fact is this, that he should write well, without knowing that he is effecting a good deal by his involved reasoning. After a similar fashion, it happens, that the perception of a subtle effect on the part of the reader, as well as of the writer, while it is always positive, and matches a definite antecedent, does not necessarily involve the formulating of the antagonist position from which it is a rebound. At the same time, a process of rapid mediation does go on in the adjusting of subtle effects—which forms a distinctive mode of syllogising. To speak of re-entrant angles as "tedious," for example, is subtle. What we bargained for in the inclusion of the re-entrant angle was its *intricacy*, which we find quite safe, *plus* the idea of wearisomeness, with a trifle of carriage to pay for the additional hint. Our knowledge of the first has been employed to mediate the conception of the second. Accordingly, this is the rationale of the stylic syllogism :—

Re-entrant angles are tedious.
Since—1 They are intricate.
And forsooth—1 All that is intricate is tedious.

And correspondingly in the negative case. The progress is from the singular, through the particular, to the universal; and consists rigorously in making explicit what in the subject was implicit.

Cor.—The second and third formulæ in both branches of the scheme, as finally explicated, admit each of a twofold mode of phrasing. For example, all P, as against some P, may be read, either as restricting the inclusion of the subject, and expanding the implication of the predicate, or else as expanding the implication of the former, and restricting the inclusion of the latter. But secondly, the universal in the first section, and the singular in the second, are identical as to phrasing, in either of these relations; and correspondingly, the singular of the first section is identical in form with the universal in the second. Accordingly, the formulæ reduce themselves to four. But thirdly, the remaining universal and singular are really functions of the particular, the one in the positive, the other in the negative relation. For, having been accustomed to think, good soul, that some S (viz. P) was Q, I am naturally surprised to learn that "any S may be Q," as, for example, X & Y. Or conversely, having been used to associate X & Y with Q, among other members of S, I am horrified to discover that, P only being Q, they are now *disimplicated* in relation to Q, *i.e.* that "any S is not Q." The variation, therefore, in either case (negative or positive), being a differential variation, and since the universal and singular may each be expressed in terms of the implication of the predicate, and the inclusion of the subject, the generic or representative formula for subtlety in a proposition is this:

that it turns upon the differential inclusion of the subject, as expounded by the differential implication of the predicate.

14.

Subtlety may appear in three forms, in a proposition, in a term (which is a condensed form of the proposition), or in the link between two propositions (which is an expanded form of the proposition). Now the terms and the propositions have this in common, that each is concerned either with a fact, a principle, or an analogy. In regard to the term, for example, we have the word "fool," to express a fact, "doltish," to express the principle or tendency, and "donkey," to express the analogy. And in the proposition, after its own method, we express the fact, by saying that such and such a man is a fool, or doltish, or a donkey; the principle, by saying that all people who sit long with damp feet are fools, doltish, etc.; and the analogue, by saying that such and such a person looked like a donkey—which is precisely the distinction between metaphor and simile, the one belonging to the term, the other to the proposition.

1. In the realm of Fact; and according to the principle of Attention. (1) There is the order of cases, in which the mind simply reproduces individual phenomena, with no activity beyond what is needed to make these significant. Thus (a) in the relation of the universal, the expression, applied to the bee, of "velvet"—because, being in the first place recondite (i.e. not such as most men would explicate to themselves), it applies to all bees, and so enhances differentially the perception of the individual who does explicate the idea, seeing that other people, from the very commonness of the fact, have just as much opportunity for

explicating it as he. (b) In the region of the particular, the expression,

> *Grape-green* all the waves are,

is subtle, just for the converse reason, viz. that the effect thus painted is comparatively rare, and, therefore, evasive. All waves are not green, nor all green waves grape-green. (c) In the relation of the singular :—

> Yonder bee anon
> Muffles low hum in some campanula
> Of nectared amethyst, *and hums again.*

That applies only to the bee. The noise of a blue-bottle, gratuitously hushed on a window-pane, is a very different thing. This has all the effect of accident, with all the sanction of necessity. (2) Subtlety in the reproduction of fact arises from the *activity* of the mind in relation to the phenomena, so as to produce a result that is true, but hypostatised. (a) By way of negatively hypostatising the collateral facts, *e.g.* to speak of the sea-beach as

> Kissed by wavelets *by winds forsaken.*

(b) By way of abstracting from the real totality of the facts, *e.g.*

> Green lizards glance among the sunbaked stones,
> Or rest at gaze with shoulder on the stone
> *And half their shadow,*

where there is a very quiet oblivion of the other, and, as the poet perhaps whispers maliciously to himself, the better half. (c) By way of integrating the conception to something more than it appears. Thus a writer describes the ox :—

> Audibly ruminating, *couch'd at ease*
> *Upon his shadow,* in a luminous moon.

Q

The idea naturally attached to shadow is that obscuration which may be seen—which demands some space intermediate between the object and the surface on which the shade is projected. So that what the animal seems to lie upon is precisely *not* its shadow. Now the poet has a perfect sanction, from the natural science point of view, to speak as he does. Only, and quite apart from that, he produces artistically an effect appreciable by all in extending the ground-shadow, so as to make it bounded on either side by light, and not on the one side by light, and on the other by the shade on the animal—in extending the unilluminated space from what we see to what (though it exists) we do not and never shall see. (3) Subtlety in the portraiture of fact may show itself in realising to the reflection truth that is actual and complex. (*a*) In the selection of an accidental relation or complexity :—

> From the sails the dew did drip—
> Till clomb above the eastern bar
> The hornèd moon, *with one bright star*
> *Within the nether tip.*

There is such a thing in what is casual as profound verisimilitude, for it is just the fortuitous which is the constant in all natural phenomena. (*b*) In the portrayal of a reflex agency :—

> Those angel forms—
> Such blush their grain of pinion warms
> *As in a milk-white lily glows,*
> *Leaned over by a lovelit rose ;*

and (*c*) in the expression of relief, as here :—

> And then away the toddler flew
> To bury her wee face where covert grew
> Of marestail and of fern, *a forest small*
> *Within the forest,* taller than them all.

2. In the realm of Principle, and according to the canon of Reason. By principle, I mean relation substantial and philosophic; whose various orders are embraced within the following schema:—

Relation.
Origination.
Mediation.
Resultance.

Disrelation.	Correlation.
Transcendence.	Community.
Adversation.	Reciprocity.
Approximation.	Convertibility.

Subtlety of mediation, which is the central conception of the first group, may be illustrated from the syllogism, which is expressly the formulating of a conclusion regarding one proposition, through the medium of another. This paragraph affords a fine example of subtlety (under the category of origin), in discerning the secret source and motive of a certain symbolic treatment:—" It has been said that the fawn belongs to Apollo and Diana, because stags are sensitive to music. But I have myself no doubt, that in this particular relation to the gods of morning, it always stands as the symbol of wavering and glancing motion on the ground, as well as of the light and shadow through the leaves, chequering the ground as the fawn is dappled."[1] Here the commonplace explanation, relying upon a principle that is sometimes subtler than that of the eye, but which in this case is too remote and visionary, is easily overthrown by a reference drawn from the more obvious sense. And in fact, an absolute proof, unique in character and in dignity, is given of the truth of the latter rendering,

[1] Mr. Ruskin.

by an expression in a poem[1] published a short time
previously :—

> " And as they leave her in the rain,
>   A milk-white doe she often fed
> Through the dim forest limps in pain
>   To lean its head
> Upon the harsh grave-wall and die.
>   More sweet to it than dells of green,
> Where mate and fawn *sun-dappled* lie,
>   Thy grave, Kathleen ! "

The effect of transcendence (in the second group of categories) is always produced by a result that has apparently
broken .loose from its mediation, and whose factors it requires a little reflection to rally. Thus :—" If a luminous
body were to be struck out of existence twelve millions of
miles away, an observer would still see it for a minute after
its extinction." And, in mathematics, the principle of
approximation is perfectly exemplified in the asymptote of
a curve, which obviously holds the relations of transcendence and adversation resolved in itself.   In the
relations of the circle and the ellipse (under the general
category of correlativity), we have a subtle illustration of
the principle of community. There the coincidence—the
describing of equal areas by the radius vector in equal
times—is expounded by the differences—the equidistance
from the centre, in the one case, as against the varying
distance in the other, and the uniform velocity of the one
moving body, as against the varying velocity of the other.
A frequent way for the principle of reciprocity to manifest
itself is under these three forms, (1) of positive correspondence, (2) of negative, and (3) of inverse correspondence ;

[1] " Kathleen," in " Beatrice, and other Poems," by the Hon. Roden Noel.

which may be illustrated from one example. In the first
instance, it may be said that the more a people abhors
crime, the more it punishes it. But in the second instance,
the fact arises to neutralise that, viz. that the mitigation of
punishment "does not result from a laxer, but an exacter
estimate of law and justice. It is *because* the many so cor-
rectly regard the law, that we can afford to punish less the
few who err." And hence, thirdly, "that is the circumstance that explains the apparent paradox, the more a
people abhors crime, the less it punishes it,"—the readiness
to punish, and the necessity to punish, moving inversely as
each other. A certain form of dialectic will exemplify the
principle of conversion. It is easy to construct such
examples. Thus we may say, it is a universal rule, that
there is no rule without exception; obviously, therefore,
one rule must be excepted, as having no exception, and as
being itself the exception to the general rule; which rule,
however, is just the universal rule first named (it being the
rule which has no exception), viz. that there is no rule
without exception. It excepts itself in the very moment of
expressing itself, *i.e.* is at once the rule and the exception,
alternately and *convertibly* either.

3. In the realm of Analogy, and according to the canon
of Fancy. (1) Subtlety underlies the differential completeness of the coincidence between type and thing
typified, *e.g.*

There is beauty in the long-ribb'd hills, in the valley soft and green,
In the *trees that stand like sages with their shadow all between,*

expressing first, the towering dignity and inevitable calm
beneficence of great minds; next, the extent of their individual overshadowing influence; and finally, the continuity

in the influence of each—it is "shadow," not shadows—
interblending with that of his neighbour. (2) There is an
order of effects, whose subtlety consists in the partial
coincidence of the symbol with what is symbolised, and
where the points of non-coincidence are hinted:—

> A wild bee in a dim chapelle,
> Hovering near a flower-bell,
> With a drowsy murmur droning,
> Imitates a priest intoning,
> With his lowly eyes intant
> Upon the Holy Sacrament.

The salient points of resemblance are these: first, in regard
to the sound, as being subdued and continuous; secondly,
in regard to the solitariness of the sound, it being the only
voice heard amid the surrounding and expectant silence;
thirdly, in regard to the sound as prelusive to the feast, and
ceasing with it.   Again, the points of contrast are, first, the
suggestion of a festive and secular purpose, as compared
with the devotional; secondly, the suggestion of isolation
and self-ministry, as compared with the distributive office
of the priest; and thirdly, the fact, that with the bee the
feast which the sound preludes is merely one of many
rapidly succeeding each other, one that ceases, expressly to
be renewed, while in the other case, it is only occasional,
and ceases, expressly that its influence may be diffused
along the intervals.   (3) There is the case in which
subtlety of affect arises from the utter antagonism between
the symbol and the substantial idea which is typified.

> As two spent swimmers that do cling together
> And choke their art.—

What do we gain from that expression ? Why, that two
friendly parties have inopportunely leagued themselves

together, to their mutual disadvantage. Now, in fact, it is
the reverse that is meant: the expression is used of enemies
in battle. Nor is this a case like the last, where the image
is divided within itself, and suggests collateral contrast;
the simile takes off at the very root of the coincidence; as
may easily be proved, for discard it from its connection
with foes in conflict, and immediately it finds a perfect
antitype in the idea of friends in distress "leagued together,"
etc., while if you divorce the other image, with all its train
of coincidences and non-coincidences, what antitype will
you find to suit it?

Cor.—The degree of subtlety varies according to different
principles. A very complex effect, of course, is produced by
a subtle combination of propositions, each in itself subtle, and
with an involution of subtlety in the phrasing. The effect,
again, may arise from the aggregation of suggestions in one
image, thus:—

Still flames of window, long and thin,

descriptive of the stained glass window-divisions in a cathedral—"long and thin," to call up the stripling look of such
divisions, "flames," to call up their pointed form, quite as
much as the glow of colour, and "still," partly to indicate the
sanctuary peace, and partly to impose a significant limitation
on the "flames." That last effect is, therefore, a complex one.
Again, a subtle principle may be superadded to an image
already subtle from its completeness, as in the expression, used
in speaking of a futile effort, that it is "an attempt to paw
the horizon." The conception is of infinite force, not only
on account of the physical impossibility (since the horizon
recedes just as the animal approaches), but metaphysically,
because "horizon" is virtually an abstraction, and to speak of

pawing it, therefore, pretty much as if one should speak of
being first cousin to the equator, or having a pair of trousers
measured for the ecliptic. A conspicuous order of subtlety,
too, is that where the reflex or complex principle is enhanced
by the delicacy of the form or material :—

> Eyelash so *frail, inlay with trail*
> *Of shade* her eyes, a maze of sweetness !
> My soul sinks through their dimlit blue
> To find in them her own completeness—

as if each eyelash left its separate impress of shade, and (as
the " trail " hints) were fringed off in the shading.

15.

Every subtle truth is essentially paradoxical, *i.e.* it bears, on
its first consideration, a different value from that which it
bears on reflection.   It is, at least, abrupt, and possibly sub-
versive of some existing conception.   Occasionally it divides
mankind into two classes, those to whom the suggestion is
startling, and those to whom it is contradictory.   Possibly it
ranges all under the latter category, as did the discovery of
the earth's motion round the sun.   That was a total contradiction of everybody's experience.   Not, however, an absolute :
the senses were not affronted, as if they had been told that
there was no motion in the circumstances at all.   For manifestly, if the earth did revolve—not sidle, but turn upon its
axis—round the sun, the very same phenomenon would be
produced; the one hypothesis, for the reflecting mind, was
just as consonant with the facts as the other, and by much
the more exciting.   The popular mind, and the mind educated
up to a certain point, are often alike inconsistent in this
respect; at one time believing statements just on account of
their paradox, and at another, disbelieving them for their

paradox. The educated person repudiates the popular idea,
that a man may be lighter just after his dinner than he was
before it; but in the same moment he revolts from the not
very unobvious truth, that any two pure abstractions (such as
Being and Non-Being) are identical, as a lie, or if not, a snare,
and if not a snare, a joke. These inconsistencies, nevertheless,
go according to a principle, which it would not be difficult to
frame, so as to anticipate and neutralise the essentially vulgar
and discreditable kind of testimony, in regard to certain questions, which is derived from majorities. Meantime, the more
commonplace the mind, the less does it value pure originality,
and the more, confounding what is merely fresh with what is
original, does it tend to undervalue the latter by comparison.
For *imaginative* synthesis the populace has no sympathy whatever, and for dialectical truth in particular, as much adaptation as a cow has for getting through a turnstile.

A man cannot be said to have subtlety for his differentia
in style, unless he is equal to a sustained originality in
thinking. Everybody says something subtle now and
again: the dice must occasionally turn out as if the experts
had loaded them. And the modes of thus reaching subtle
truth are just the modes of the expert, only they are not
employed so continuously, or upon the same fields. Subtlety is never more transcendental than *reflection;* and a
truth *is* only subtle for those who can fully apprehend it.
It would be inaccurate, therefore, to speak of a thing unintelligible, as absolutely subtle; much rather a suggestion is
absolutely subtle, which is perfectly intelligible, and a truth
not quite intelligible is only relatively subtle, because it can
be valued only indirectly. By reflection, therefore, it is
that such effects are attained; and often through a man's

discarding his first impressions, or reverting to those which
forsooth he had discarded for others which have now to be
relinquished as false. Subtlety is not always a second-sight,
that raises a man, as if inspired, above his fellows, but often
a second sight in the coarse numerical sense. Thus an
author, in speaking of a death by drawing asunder, remarks
that the victim was torn "by antagonist, yet confederate
forces"; where he shows the maximum of reflective power,
since in "confederate" he has given the very antithesis of
his primary drift; and yet he has only exhibited a power of
fanciful reflection, after all.

Cor.—No man is truly original who is not also subtle to his
finger-ends. But no perception is really subtle, unless it is
also true. And in proportion as the speculative truth in the
world has been brought out by individuals, in that proportion
is it indebted to subtlety. That subtlety should be regarded
as necessarily equivocal, arises in part from this, that men
take pleasure in certain forms of it, without thinking earnestly
of its allied truth; or even charge the pleasure, attendant on
the perception of the truth, to the account of the other; and
so come to regard subtle suggestion as a medium of amusement,
not of work—of information and reformation. Nor is this
mode merely to be regarded as one of the ways of attaining
certain truths: there are truths—and truth in many instances
lies on the farther side of a quicksand—which cannot be
attained in any other way. Of which the most natural proof
is in the immediate case of subtlety itself: how should the
truth on that question be attained without subtlety? It
cannot possibly be attained otherwise, any more than minute
atmospheric changes can be registered, except by an apparatus
correspondingly delicate. Subtlety here becomes an instru-

ment as technical as the barometer; and thus the necessity
for it is demonstrated, precisely in those regions where
its application is most pertinent and unique. And in
literature, subtlety is not applicable to anything but what is
true, whether poetical or scientific. To deny the existence of
the external world, therefore, by affirming it to be an affection
of the senses, etc., is more offensive than the most putrid
commonplace. So to speak of the sun, in poetry, as " burn-
ing without beams," is pure nonsense, and in the spurious
maudlin oriental style of expression. Contrast with that the
unaffected rendering of a natural fact in the lines:—

> Dimples, here and there,
> That insects dint with long-legged stride.

Everybody knows that what distinguishes a ripple from a wave
is the twitching up of the skin of the water, as it were, under
the wind. Now as a wave is to a ripple, so is the plash of a
stone to the dimple of the water by the limb of an insect: the
plunge goes beyond dinting. But to the limber touch of the
fly, the surface of the water, so easily shattered by the plunge
of a stone, merely undergoes a shiver or flicker; and the
expression "dint" conveys precisely the momentary impression upon the impervious elastic surface of the pool.
The image is subtle, is poetical, just because it is so loudly
scientific in its truth. The true mode of a man's power, who
has such sensibility to natural effects, it may take a genera-
tion fully to appreciate, even for his fidelity of perception, so
long as people see with their noses. But it is just this same
intensity of truth, in the midst of his characteristic subtlety
of insight, that has made our contemporary poet, Mr. Noel, in
so extraordinary a degree, the greatest among the poetical
draughtsmen and colourists of all time.

Section III.   Of Comprehensiveness.

16.

In regard to any statement, no matter whether that concerns a principle or a detail, the question arises, do its subject and predicate lawfully reciprocate ? The immediate relation here is one of truth. And the general form of such a question is this, does the subject as a whole include that specific complement of attributes which form the predicate, and do these apply in their completeness to everything that is implicated in the subject ? If that condition is fulfilled, the proposition is comprehensive. And the formula for such a quality of thought is this: *comprehensiveness in any proposition turns upon the integral inclusion of its subject, as expounded by the integral implication of its predicate.*

If the inclusion of many terms were to be explicated, their moments would appear to be very heterogeneous. Nevertheless, when once the relations of a term are fixed, it behaves according to one uniform principle. By which I do not mean, in the first instance, that every term, being a singular, must have each of its moments specifically fixed, as *either* universal or particular, and not as alternatively the one or the other, according to the proximate conception which for the moment regulates its internal significance. That, no doubt, is true : expressions must not veer or be bandied about in such a fashion. But it follows as a corollary from *this*, that every term has its own complement of inclusion ; " curiosity," for example, having on the one side, as its universal, " desire for information," and on the other " pettiness," as its particular. Now the *vitiating* of comprehensiveness arises from putting too fine or too blunt an edge upon the predicate of a proposition, using, *e.g.*, the proximate singular "prurience," instead of the subordinate singular, which stands to "prurience" for a universal, viz. "curiosity," and *vice versa*. An uncomprehensive thinker betrays himself immediately, even to people of not much general discernment; probably by a neglect of the singular, if his temperament is languid, and by an abuse of it, if his bias is impulsive. Wherever motive is concerned, there is all the chance in the world of a man's abusing the singular. COR.—The universal canon of integrity in the comprehensiveness of propositions may be variously expounded. To a certain extent, it might appear to depend on the nature of the subject treated of, whether the result were comprehensive, or the reverse. Much more, however, depends on the individual. It is better to hear a man of capacity on midges, than a noodle on the Trinity. But much depends also on the mode of writing prescribed. If you prescribe the treatment solely of details, you proscribe the very essence of a comprehensive treatment in style. Hence the second canon of *dignity*, which ordains a universal implication in the subject. Hence, too, the essential dignity of poetry, that, with the representation of a fact, it may convey a principle. This image, for example, is as purely analytic as any axiom in mathematics :—

The moonpath flecking thin and tremulous the sea,

where each expression tells like the explosion of a bomb. The more perfect such an image, the more does it supersede and disparage all other renderings of the same phenomenon. The phrase, "inlaying the sea with pearl," applied to the glimmer of the moon, is artificial, in comparison, and narrow.

But this happens, because the other is so trenchant—apart from the fact, that a literal rendering of nature-phases is necessarily more forcible than a metaphorical. Hence the canon of *felicity*, which ordains that the differentia of every subject shall be given, by deepening the inclusion of the predicate. Objection may, therefore, be taken at once to all such terms as " angelic " and " fairy-like," which are simply the most dead and ineffective of poetical mannerisms. By the side of the *finesse* that reveals itself in the expression just quoted, " fairy," applied to anything whatsoever, is lumpish, and "angel" unspiritual. Here it is precisely that the spurious, and quasi-tautological, in analytic expression is so offensive:—" But let the sober and serious hour come, which sooner or later must come to all, the power of truth will soon prove *too strong for all that can be opposed to it*, and pierce into his heart," which is pretty much the same thing as a man's saying, that D. V. he intends to shave to-morrow morning with a razor, if he cannot lay hands on anything else;— with this gross difference, that the last man must be a wag, the other is not. Thus the circle is completed. For it is the abuse of this principle which constitutes the breach of the initial principle of integrity. If the predicate includes too many attributes, it cannot be applied *in its integrity* to implicate the subject. Thus " some anachronisms are solecisms " must be altered to the universal of " solecisms," viz. " anomalies." That being accomplished, it is the turn of the subject to raise the " some " to an " all," and, by way of reversion upon that, it is for the predicate again to expand the inclusion, by assigning the differentia of anachronism, as, for example, thus : " All anachronisms are anomalous trans-positions of different events in time."

17.

Comprehensiveness may appear in two relations, besides that which it has to simple propositions. On the one hand, it may appear in the connection between propositions, and, on the other, in the connection between the clauses or sections of single propositions.

A transition is uncomprehensive when it shoots beside the mark—either over or under it. For example, it is so, when the occasion of anything is assigned as the cause. And, on the other hand, its want of comprehensiveness consists in placing together indefinitely, propositions, whose mediation, from one to the other, should be made explicit; as, for instance, in putting side by side, as parallel facts, circumstances, of which the one is the direct outcome of the other. In such a case, the writer often fails of being incisive, not because he mistrusts the severer connection, but because he does not see it at all : he does not shirk it, he misses it.

The proposition again, as divided internally, may be either a binomial, a trinomial, or a polynomial. (The mononomial relation has been discussed in the preceding paragraph.) Thus :—"Endless are the purposes of men, merely festal, or merely comic, and aiming but at the momentary life of a cloud, which have earned for themselves the distinction and apparatus of a separate art." Here, in the first clause, "festal" and comic" mark a bisection in the thought, and in the second, "distinction" and "apparatus." There is, however, an apparent trisection in the first, owing to the phrase, "and aiming," etc.; but that is the statement of a characteristic which is common to both "festal" and "comic," viz. their intrinsic levity. A perfect illustration of the threefold division is this :—

" From the first intermeddling of law with the movement
of the higher moral affections, there is an end—to freedom
in the act, to purity in the motive, to dignity in the personal relation ;" where there is given, first, the fact, next,
its origin, and finally its result. The polynomial relation
may be illustrated from this proposition :—"We glory
in tribulations also—knowing that tribulation worketh
patience, and patience experience, and experience hope, and
hope maketh not ashamed." It is not hard to discover
what is the critical point for comprehensiveness in such
propositions, or what divisions are imperfect. It does not
follow, that because a statement is broken up into sections,
it is less comprehensive than a simple statement ; although
it may happen that a threefold distribution is necessarily
more comprehensive, because more economical, than a four-
fold. What is required is, on the one hand, that the
divisions shall not be elliptical—no polite proposition ever
yawns to the extent of a third or fourth of its whole
superficies. The principle of distribution must not be blind.
On the other hand, the sections must not overlap each
other. An impetuous writer, or one who writes for impression upon the common mind, is very apt to fall into
slovenly modes of co-ordinating his ideas :—" Whatsoever
things are true, whatsoever things are honest, whatsoever
things are just, whatsoever things are pure, whatsoever
things are lovely, whatsoever things are of good report ; if
there be any virtue, and if there be any praise, think on
these things." The last clause contains a very happy
antithesis, as summing up the virtues as they are in themselves, on the one hand, and as they are *for us*, on the other.
And the same antithesis holds in the main division

of the first clause. Only there the separate phrases are
very loosely connected; since there is no fundamental
principle of division. And what holds for ordinary
thought, holds also for poetry. It is true that Shakspere
constantly multiplies metaphors; but only for the sake of
intensifying an impression, by expounding it from different
points of view, which is quite a distinct practice from trail-
ing a mass of particulars in rag-tag-and-bobtail fashion
after the main thought. For if a definite principle of
division underlies the conception, any mere details are
superfluous, and if not, they must be more or less arbitrary.

Cor.—The general appearance of a comprehensive thought
may be rendered appropriately by a very genial extension of
the term *sententious*. The sentence is the full, rounded proposition; and whatever causes a thought to assume a robust
appearance, is sententious. By the term generally is understood, whatsoever is characterised by this in excess. Accordingly all such writing is bombastic, and weak. But, in the
milder sense of the term, all good writing is sententious, more
or less; just in proportion as the thoughts of men who write
carelessly give the idea of limpness, and a want of having
come into being through resistance. Hence it happens that
so much writing is unequivocally *flat*, and wanting in relief.
It is not necessary that every thought should be epigrammatic
in its setting; but it is indispensable that it should be analytically definite. This is the fundamental order of the sententious; and accordingly there is (1) the simple proposition;
pure in the double sense of being undiluted, and free from
extraneous matter. Thus: "No man escapes the contagion
from contemporary bystanders." Of such, too, are all mathematical theorems, &c.: "The three angles of a triangle are

H

together equal to two right angles."   (2) There is the proposition, with a clause qualifying the main idea.   These sentences are formed in various ways, by augmenting, or limiting,
or simply explicating, the primary thought.   *E.g.* "Many of
the inhabitants (and all those of respectability) subscribed to
the fund."—"This is a paradox, only in the sense which makes
it honourable to be paradoxical."—"Popularly, *i.e.* amongst
the thoughtless, literature is held to include everything that is
printed in a book."   All good writing deals constantly with
the relations of facts—their aim, origin, exceptions, circumstances, adverse influences, advantages, proportions, &c., &c.
And as the vocabulary of a bad writer is indefinite, so is his
grouping.   (3) There is the proposition with an antithesis;
e.g. "The possibility of selecting books wisely is becoming
more hopeless, as the necessity for selection is becoming continually more pressing."   A certain distrust might be attached
to effects so glittering, were it not that these very effects are
most exposed to criticism, where they have the chance of
being most telling, and are most brilliant, when they found
upon such principles of reciprocity as are logically the most
just.   And what becomes thus a habit of good writing is due
to more dignified sources than literary knack and facility: it
is engrained in the thinking.   Such effects, of course, are the
most elaborate; and many men write from year to year, without striking a single antithesis.   This mode of setting the
thought gains, accordingly, by comparison, while it cannot
lose by any abuse that might be attempted.

18.

In so far as subtlety and comprehensiveness represent, the
one the differential, the other the integral, in the variation of

terms, they are formally opposed to each other. But they are
so distinguished from each other, just because they are correlative functions. The one takes up what the other leaves
undone; and where the one is active, the other is in abeyance.
But this is only true formally. And in a very obvious sense,
to integrate a term is to differentiate it, after a fashion, and to
differentiate it is to integrate it. Alter a term in any way
you please, up or down, and you must integrate its inclusion
or its implication. And at the same time you have caused
the meaning to *differ* from what it was a moment previously.
Just in the same way it happens that a writer's totality of
expression, forming an *integral* fact, becomes his *differentia* in
regard to other individual writers. So long as comprehensiveness and subtlety are looked at apart from one another, each is
seen to assume a characteristic form. But the one is involved in
the other, and in practice this involution is of exceeding power
and significance. There may be an isolated remark comprehensive, without being subtle, and *vice versa*. But there is no such
thing as *continuous* expression that is comprehensive, without
being subtle—although, of course, either quality can only be
illustrated from individual expressions—and *vice versa*. For
evidently, if everybody holds that all P is Q, you, who see
that some P only is Q, must have embraced the rejected
members of P with a grasp as comprehensive as that of any
one else, as it is certainly more pertinent than that of every
one else. And if, on the other hand, you embrace all P, as
being implicated by Q, your subtlety must have co-operated to
discover the principle upon which the outcast section of P
has been fallaciously excluded from association with Q. Each
quality is the exponent of the other.

> The cattle are grazing,
> Their heads never raising,
> There are forty feeding like one.

What have we here—an image that is more comprehensive,
or more subtle?   Subtle it is to begin with, from the sudden
combination of ideas—some P is some Q—that by and by
diffuses itself like the dawn.   For after the surprise, it is seen
that there is no straining in the predicate, no spurious refinement, or discordance.   It is at least generic in relation to
animals as opposed to non-generic, and applies comprehensively
to the subject;—some P is all Q.   But is this not merely a
vanishing picture, as applied to that predicate?   The habit
belongs, so far as we can recollect, to no other animal; but are
cattle found feeding in such fashion so frequently, as to constitute it, for them, a habit?   Surely—only some P is not
all Q.   This the comprehensiveness verifies, by summing up
the occasions on which cattle have been remembered to graze
in this manner, and mounts the proposition thus:—all P is
all Q—the predicate being a proprium, not an accident.   But
now, again, are there not other animals besides cattle, which
feed after this manner?   No;—any S is not all Q.   Sheep
feed in numbers, too, and of all animals, therefore, most
resemble cattle in that respect.   But sheep do not feed
"forty like one."   They lack the consentaneousness and
repose of a herd of cattle feeding (and what, by the way,
is the secret distinction between "flock" and "herd"?);
their motion in feeding is a twitching, rather than a
browsing; and some of them in a flock are always in
impatient motion.   This is distinction enough, and is the distinction indicated in the expression;—although the difference
to the ear in the sound made by the different animals in feed-

ing might accentuate that distinction, and even if the
spectator were removed out of hearing might associate itself
with what he sees, especially if he is sensitive to the converse
case, that, viz. of passing by a field after nightfall, when the
cattle may be heard and not seen. And this distinction the
comprehensiveness ratifies by showing the predicate to be the
differentia, not applicable to the genus :—only P is all Q.

Subtlety.	Comprehensiveness.
1. Some P is some Q.	2. Some P is all Q.
3. Only some P is not all Q.	4. All P is all Q.
5. All S is not all Q.	6. Only P is all Q.

And conversely, instead of beginning with the negation of the
proposition, no P is any Q (viz. some P is some Q), we may
begin by negating the result attained in No. 6. Thus if we
are told that only certain kinds of scientific men are the
authorities on a subject, we may demur, by suggesting (1) that
there may be others who have a claim to be heard, in fact (2)
that all scientific men have an equal claim; further that the
specialists are (3) not all competent upon the subject, but (4)
that only some of them are competent; and finally, that (5)
even these are more or less incompetent, because, as it turns
out, this subject is not their subject, but one apart, so that (6)
not one of them has a voice in the matter. Thus, the
Predicate being still quantified :—

Subtlety.	Comprehensiveness.
1. Only P is not all Q.	2. All S is all Q.
3. All P is not all Q.	4. Only some P is all Q.
5. Some P is not all Q.	6. No P is any Q.

Novelty is the hidden condition of comprehensiveness,
just as truth is its overt condition. Certain principles, just
by reason of their novelty and subtlety, tend to become
commonplace. They are at first striking, and so come to be

in everybody's mouth, with the reversionary certainty of
being the opposite of striking. In the same way it
happens with figurative expressions. The simile about the
lion shaking the dewdrops from his mane *once* was new.
And for central Africa at the present moment undoubtedly
it *is* new ; that expression being understood to bring down
the house nightly in the Theatre Royal of the Sahara.
Only by and by it will come to the ears of the lions, who
will grow sulky, and refuse to do the shake, and so the
metaphor will be no longer true. But meantime, and for
home consumption, the expression must be turned over
to the wags, who will find plenty ways of applying it,
so that it shall blossom like the apple-trees in spring.
Otherwise, such expressions, being derived, involve no comprehensiveness on the part of the writer who uses them. A
proverb is equally an exponent of comprehensiveness;
which is a form of expression professing to be comprehensive, and not subtle; though it is not always what it
professes to be, and when it is, that happens because it is
subtle as well, *i.e.* is that which it does not profess to be.

Cor.—Considered psychologically, and in a strict scientific
sense, it is the union of subtlety and comprehensiveness
which constitutes genius. The term may be used vulgarly to
denote anything, from heat and clap-trap to a rhythmical
felicity that is comparatively mechanical ; and may be bent
to suit a variety of descriptions, which are simply not quack
definitions, because they do not pretend to be scientific. The
term, as commonly used, is itself equivocal. A writer may
quite well be distinct from the crowd, who is yet not to be
classed with men of the highest power ; and would not be so
classed, even by those who confound under the one term

catholic power, and power that is merely eccentric. The men of true power have a bond drawing them together, and isolating them from men of the second class, *plus* their individuality. It is not individuality alone that constitutes genius. For manifestly, if A, B, and C, are all men of genius, there must be something *common* amongst them, just as if they are Chinese, there must be something common to them all, whether they wear pigtails or not. In itself, individuality is the most barren criterion that can be conceived; for being, in the abstract, common to them all, it denudes each of the writers of his common, *concrete* power; each man's individuality excludes that of his neighbour. That being the case, the distinction of genius between the mind of high originality and the ordinary mind, is just as peremptory between it and the middle-men or eccentrics. Which distinction is something of a definite intellectual cast. It is, therefore, co-present with genial power of whatever kind; and that not merely as an accompaniment, but as a substratum. No emotion can possibly be gauged, can possibly express itself in literature, except through some intellectual medium. Its force and delicacy are expounded by its comprehensiveness and subtlety. Nor is this a task to which language is unequal. Communication of such emotion, now ethereal, now masculine, is made every day; and with this proof of the infallibility of the medium, that *all* who read do not respond to the feeling, or respond to it in different degrees. Those who are affected by it are precisely those of whom we could predict that they should be affected; and those who are not, are precisely those in whom we have seen the want of capacity for appreciating it. The influence of emotion is, therefore, manifestly regulated by principle, precisely because it is not indiscriminate. It

might be thought, that the fact of a man's not having seen the
emotional force of a passage, and apprehending it, upon re-
reading the piece, were a proof of the insecurity of this mode
of communication. It is in fact the very opposite; the mood
simply has not been favourable at first for catching the
peculiar sentiment; and the mode of transit would indeed be
precarious if, when the emotions were inert, the piece *had*
been adequately apprehended. Hence it is, that the reader
recurs to the passage with undiminished pleasure. All of
which depends upon the permanence of the intellectual co-
efficients. It is not merely that these include the principles
of poetical genius, but that they allow for genius of the philosophic and scientific cast, as well as of the poetical;—and here
is another source of equivocation, since so few people can
square the idea of poetical genius with scientific, and most
people when they talk of genius mean distinctively the former.
The power, therefore, as not merely (1) concrete, and to be
found in a man's individual expressions, but (2) specifically
intellectual and constant, is (3) essentially recoverable by
analysis, and to be measured in detail. It does not follow that
because comprehensiveness and subtlety are not to be
predicated of a man's style from single expressions, his genius
can be determined without appraising these expressions. It
is predicable in detail, provided you predicate in regard to a
sufficient number of details. And just because it is so, the
caution needs to be given at all regarding isolated expressions.
These appear as particulars, and form the universal which we
call genius, which, in so far, is *not* local or individual; only
the specific form which realises the genius of each man in its
individuality, is just that mode of expression under which the
common element incarnates itself, in art and science.

CHAPTER III.

OF QUANTITY.

Section I. The Principle of Quantity.

19.

A VERY important distinction exists in Style between thoughts
as they are independently, and the same thoughts in a process.
It holds both in relation to single propositions and to proposi·
tions in a series. So that, on the one hand, a series of thoughts
may be regarded as containing propositions separately intelligible; and, on the other, separate propositions may be regarded
in relation to mutual reticulation or coherence, each of them
being potentially a link or item in a series. For the distinctness or completeness of an idea is as necessary for progress as
for positive disconnection—which in fact is just the difference
between insulation and isolation: dig a trench across the home
end of a peninsula, and you insulate it; wash away the island
now formed, from the side of the canal, till its diameter is less
than the distance which divides it from the mainland, and
you isolate it. And this progression to an indefinite extent,
with transitions more or less severe and artistic, and ap·
pealing more or less to a chain of unexpressed connection, reposes upon a natural tendency to the evolution, more
or less systematic, of one thought through the medium of
another.

I

I apprehend that a person asked to discourse to an audience on landscape-gardening may formulate his subject as he pleases, may select for his text a fact, or a proposition, or a series of propositions, and may deliver accordingly an essay, a thesis, or a lecture. But, in either case, his very first movement towards an elucidation or confirmation of his theme is a departure from the position he has assumed. He cannot expound his subject by simply reiterating the phrase " landscape-gardening." He must proceed by beginning somewhere else. If he is simply obtuse, he will begin with a few general remarks on the interesting nature of the art. If he is pretentious as well as obtuse, he will grasp at futile analogies in the subject to landscape-painting, led thither by the coincidence of the term, and proceed to splice the two subjects according to the correspondence which he has chipped smooth for them. If he is a master, he will sever the subject in its differentia from the generic science of gardening, with a hint of its leaning to landscape to convey its affinities to the picturesque as well as the stubbornly useful in art. Nor does this happen from the common usage with regard to introductions and exordia. On the contrary, these are possible only through this principle of quantity; they derive their proportion to the whole theme entirely from it; and their abuse arises through an unseasonable extension of its peculiar functions. Not one of the propositions in the series may contain an expression implicating any of the terms in the text, and yet the whole may be a perfect exposition of it. Or the terms themselves may be expressed in every proposition of the discourse, and no illustration given of it whatever. Universally, therefore, it holds, that the secession of the expositor from his first posi-

tion is the first condition of his return to it; the fact being
that the thesis, which henceforth is his *terminus ad quem*,
is, for the moment of its being stated, his *terminus a quo*.

COR.—The practical conditions of all interesting thought are
two, that it shall explicate truth, or make it impressive. In
the one case, the communicator takes advantage of the obscurity of a principle, in the other of its simplicity; or rather
he lessens or remedies the disadvantage attaching on the one
hand to a truth that is profound, and on the other to one that
is commonplace. Now to set the truth in its relations cannot
be effected for either aim, unless he causes the parts of his
exposition in detail to be apprehended mediately through each
other. And since the separate propositions must precede or
succeed one another in time, priority and subsequence become
the exponent of relation in thought. For its own part, the
principle overlooks all difference in the importance of individual thoughts. One idea may be worth in quality of suggestion all the rest put together; or it may be the sole unfertile
thought in a series that is massively and resplendently suggestive. Its value for transition may or may not coincide
with its intrinsic and independent value.

20.

By whatsoever laws of sequence in fact, or of analogy, or of
logical consequence, a thought has reached its position in a
series, it is the rule, that the truth which for the time being
occupies the attention shall have an advantage over every
other—an advantage immediate, in the way of excluding
every other, an advantage derivative, in the way of suggesting
others. It is a supplanter of every other truth to this extent,
that any truth supplanting it shall do so only in virtue of the

relation of that truth to itself the proximate truth. Ab-
dicating the throne, it has a right to name its successor; the
chances being that this will be a relative, according to its
force at the moment of resignation. That a certain range of
thought has been in occupation for some time is a pre-
sumption that it will soon be displaced; its displacement, in
fact, is rapidly being carried on. For each idea has two distinct values, a potential value, as a generating or multiplying
source of ideas, and an actual, as a link in the development
of a succession of ideas. The potential value, therefore, of
such a chain of thought is being reduced with every successive proposition to actual value. And correspondingly its
power of resistance to a possible succeeding series of thoughts
is being reduced to zero—a process that, with discontinuous
thinkers, goes on very rapidly.

The two factors requisite for systematic composition are
physical energy and intellectual fertility. Nor will their
conjoint operation be defeated, except on the suspension
of the conditions under which the initial thought was
generated. That suspension will be a mixed result from
physical exhaustion, and a lack of that surplus fund of
unorganized suggestions regarding the immediate theme,
precisely to the extent that the potential energy, or the
potential fund of illustration, has had demands made upon
it. The resistance, in such a case, to the production of
fresh thought would certainly be enormous. In fact, writing under such circumstances is quite exceptional. It is,
however, the ordinary case which I contemplate, and precisely the opposite circumstances, viz., those in which
the resistance arises from the tumult and redundancy of
the thought. For every new idea operates by way of dis-

turbing existing relations. If these have been exhausted, it does not come a moment too soon. If not, it acts in the way either of delaying the development of the thought, or of precipitating it. A resistance has, in fact, been interposed which it was beyond its province to interpose, arising from weakness or impatience. And there are two factors, as *powers*, which are affected by a want of distribution of energy in the mental powers—the powers of suggestion and modulation; so that it is not so much they that are disturbed, as the process of combination which is disturbed, because they do not act in harmony. The fault may be a defect in either case. Or it may be an abnormal activity of the suggestive faculty, the elaborative faculty not being able to weave into shape the materials as they are passed back to it. Not that by any means this activity could be represented as so much surplus energy. It is the same force applied momentarily in a different direction; and viciously applied, because it is not distributed so as to sustain the modulating agency. Such action of the imagination is simply spasmodic, and just as much a sign of vigour as tetanus might be of muscular power. It is not enough, therefore, that the writer's force is at its maximum, it must also be, as to its two factors, *in equilibrio*. With diminished total energy a finer result will be attained, than with increased energy disproportionately applied. The moment any plethora is felt, the diastole begins to remedy the disturbance and restore the diminishing clearness. Otherwise not merely will some of the suggestions founder, but the elements which were about to consolidate in their totality will be dispersed. To obviate that, a cessation of the process is necessary, and a revision, to the extent that the attention has failed in its first effort to meet its extra engagements—has failed to neutralize the resistance offered by the difficulties of the process augmented by the difficulties of the situation. The two functions must again concur in amending the relations of the thought to their mutual satisfaction. And they will do so in the converse order from that in which they concurred to fashion the combination which now they are called upon to reconstitute; each in that ratio being called out or withheld, in which, for the original draught, it had unduly been depreciated or exalted.

Cor.—This tendency to disturbance exists in all composition, even the most negligent. And, properly controlled, it is the very springboard of effective composition. It is felt, therefore, most decidedly in the experience of the best writers, who precisely are those born with the best resources for managing it. A writer who has the advantage of a thinking that is highly complex, must share its partial disadvantages for rapid improvisation. His tendency is to involve fresh suggestions with every turn of his argument. But counterworking that, and with a view to the summary extinction of those interminable ramifications, which make it oftentimes uncertain what is the leading idea, is a regulative faculty, moving abreast of the tumultuary flux of ideas, and determining what phases of the thought are to be rejected, what subordinated, and what reserved for a more special expansion in arrear. His resource lies in the exceptional rapidity with which he is able to pass from the final adjustment of a thought to the rehearsal of an impending thought, and from the pioneer stage back into the complementary one of adjustment.

21.

The correspondences, which take effect in the relations of the suggestive and regulative faculties during composition, are founded on the reciprocity of relation between Quantity and Quality. It is self-evident, that you cannot connect two ideas unless they have some common tenor and significance (their quality), or, on the other hand, expound that relationship, unless both, and in their individuality (their numerical distinctness, their quantity), be co-present. For example, a historian, treating of the causes of a revolution, sums them up in three propositions. This has been accomplished by their mutual relevance, depending ultimately on their separate significance; which has been the agency in limiting them to that precise number as a maximum. The quality in this instance has determined the quantity. Suppose, however, that there could not have been less than three. In that case the effect depends upon the comprehensiveness of each of the three propositions; and quantity has become the exponent of quality. For if another writer requires a larger compass to produce three truths of equal dimensions, if his complete truths only alternate with partial truths, it is evident that the other is the more comprehensive thinker. If you allow an author to unite two propositions separately obvious, you may produce a subtle result. For by showing its unexpected relation to a principle, he may have glorified a fact which was commonplace, and even the principle, by developing unexpectedly its wealth of application. Or conversely, by reading into connection with other truths a truth that in isolation was original, you may make it commonplace. This proposition: "Fathers of the church are no more to be relied on as authorities in doctrine than lay authors," is docked considerably as to its impressiveness by a preceding statement: "There have been many heterodox professors of divinity and freethinking bishops." The function of quantity is thus precisely to determine the *variation* of quality. For when I say that the one expounds the other, I do not mean by way of illustrating its brilliance; but simply that it enforces the other, whether in the way of magnifying or depreciating it—of showing it up as subtle or non-subtle, just according as it is either.

It is a most significant truth, that condensation is a test of high thinking, and for the profound reason, that it depends in such great measure on the quality of the thinking. An accidental advantage, therefore, it is not; nor one arising where, we might imagine, it could best be dispensed with; but one arising from necessity, since it is precisely vast combinations that are the most subtle, exquisite transitions that are the most just. A great writer is dissatisfied with such relations as do *not* cause his meaning to subtend a definite angle in the preceding thought. The inferior writer has usages of transition known only to himself. When he is at a loss for a connection, he simply couples his ideas formally together as one, two, three, without troubling himself to ascertain what cross-division he may have made, or whether there is any coherence in his chain of thought at all. Strictly speaking, these are transitions only in the sense that creeping is walking. That he does not write very much absolute nonsense is just owing to this, that he evades definite logical forms of articulating his thoughts. It is not that, having to use the looser forms of transition, he has no occasion for those that are more severe, but that, being illogical, he instinctively evades them. For confine him entirely to these formulæ, and you will find not that he braces himself up correspondingly to wield them, but that he will commit himself more than ever; so closely does the sharpness of a man's transitions depend upon his logical sagacity. Making an infrequent use of certain forms of combination in his ordinary composition, he makes inevitably a disproportionate use of those which remain; thus inverting the practice of all conscientious artists, which is to apply with discrimination the most telling transitions, by continually turning over the whole complement of transitions.

COR.—The functions of Quantity and Quality, in their interconnection, form the essential principle of what we mean by Style. The varieties of imagery and mood are quite secondary. It is not that these primary distinctions are abstract principles, on which the others may rest theoretically; nor merely that they are vital functions, with which the varieties of expression may coalesce and interpenetrate. They are superlative *facts* in all composition. The more catholic, therefore, a style is—the more it relies upon sound and original thinking, and rapid precision of movement—the less it is imitable; in part, because it is wanting in the mere vividness and the mere agility of the secondary attributes of expression (and which alone can be imitated), and in part because it depends on an organic force that is incommunicable. Hence another secret of the vulgarity of imitation; for a man can only copy that which is extra-essential, whether existing in or out of connection with what is really vital. Hence, too, the utter impotence of charging plagiarism upon a style that resembles another, so long as the coincidence is in the cardinal functions; as if by possibility any writer

could counterfeit a manner that is essentially inimitable, and
as if it were not a libellous misreading of his independent
merits to suppose him coveting what, being incommunicable
from himself, he must first have divorced from his own
manner in order to counterfeit.

Section II. Of Extension.

22.

Since the proposition is for Style the unit of length, it
must internally be complete. Directly or indirectly it takes
part in propagating the thought; and *ex hypothesi* is an
integral portion of the whole series. Every such unit,
whether disinterestedly, and for the welfare of the series, or
selfishly, and as having a stake in the total application of the
line of thought, is compelled to be distinct, and to realise a
specific identity, with whatsoever detail it may be expressed
in the text, or in whatsoever variety of form it might otherwise be expressed. There can be no range of thought so great,
as to extend the unit of length in proportion, nor any so short,
as to diminish the necessity for insulating each proposition.

The onus of bearing the thought may be shared by the
subordinate members of a proposition, but only in so far as
they help to preserve its unity. It need not be simple;
but it must be single. This unity is the necessity for
expression, into whatever complexity a thought may run.
A man may wish to compose a sentence of hyperbolical
length, but unless he writes nonsense he does not lose the
unity; so long as he continues to add to the sentence,
he is simply deferring it; and his subordinate ideas themselves will be capable each of being explicated into a
totality similar to that which he is seeking to evade.

COR.—As the basis of Quality in Style is the same as that of logical Quantity, so *the basis of Quantity in Style is identical with that of Quality in Logic.* Every thought fully mounted for transition has first a distinct meaning, in order that it may have a direction, or what is technically called a drift, whether it is to be regarded as a synthesis of compatible elements, or a disjunction of elements that analytically are involved in each other. Every proposition depends, therefore, for its coherence on the *copula,* no matter whether that be negative or positive.

23.

The principle of movement in composition is from one complete proposition to another, and so on indefinitely, provided the nexus is preserved between each. Every proposition thus becomes alternately complementary to that which precedes and that which follows. The two conditions of this movement are, positively, that of advance, and, negatively, that of connection. Mere succession without connection is not progress. Discoursing on it matters not what, I announce, first, " that in savage times men are much more liable wantonly to provoke each other to bloodshed than in civilised times," and, next, " that we are at present in the middle of harvest." Now a first thought, in relation to any theme whatsoever, is excused from being directly in connection, on the express understanding that it will take the first chance of ingratiating itself with something that will lead it into that connection. Instead of that, in this instance, it is as far from the possible theme as ever, and, together with proposition No. 2, the exponent of a principle that would reduce all expression to a series of detached remarks, relevant to nothing, and as rigorously introductory to nothing. The position of the thought is constantly shifting, and so rapidly, as to make it impossible to say at what angle the new idea meets the old. The vice of the case lies in its being merely the repetition of the *initial principle*. We do not advance, simply because we are always beginning; and, unless we connect, we never get beyond that beginning.

But it does not follow, on the other hand, that if we state the same proposition over again with a little variation, we are fulfilling the law of connection which is outraged in setting side by side two disjunct ideas. For in such a case it is evidently the minimum of variation which ought to be aimed at. And it is impossible to multiply to any extent the circumstantial variations of the same substantial thought, even if that were of any use. But this is just what is demanded, viz., that the same idea shall be reiterated indefinitely (short of absolute repetition), so as not to encroach upon the identity of any other thought. Now certain thoughts allow of no permutation; absolute truths have little patience for being tampered with. And the writer will find that, with every succeeding change of his capital theme, he is further from the identity he had agreed to preserve, and more and more in league with the difference which he was committed to avoid. So far, in fact, from evading the impropriety of advance without connection —which was proved to consist in repeating merely the initial impulse—this is a gross aggravation of it, the truth being that the initial movement is repeated, and with staleness of matter superadded to sameness of principle.

An abrupt transition is quite a common thing in writing. Thus: "The prisoners having no other refuge, saw one in the sea. The weltering billows might at least hide them

from their enemies; those hellish faces through the gather-
ing mists of death they might at least shut out. Not so:
not thus were they to be dismissed. The Syrian sea is an
inhospitable chamber of the great central Christian lake."
Understood in its possible relation to what goes before, this
last sentence, so abrupt, cannot have any reference to the
change of death as affected by the volition of the prisoners.
If drown these wretches must, the more turbulently hostile
the sea, the better—the more in secret friendly to their
melancholy purpose, the more solicitous to their despairing
mood. The sentence, therefore, can only indicate either
compassion on the part of the captors, or sarcasm on the
writer's part at their meditating some more elaborately
cruel form of death for the prisoners than suffering them to
drown themselves. In the context, however, it runs:—
"Nothing rose to view but a barren rock," to which, in the
sequel, the captives swam out; and being recalled under
promises of amnesty for the past, were treacherously
massacred. The reference points onward, then, to the
sheltering rock, not to the devouring waves—the sea was
hospitable to the extent of providing a rock; and it was in
spite of its general inhospitality, and not because of it, that
the catastrophe was deferred. The transition is virtually
the same with the principle of the initial movement in
any piece of composition. Meantime, its relation to
what succeeds is certain; and it is only by picking
up the connection to windward of the spot where the
thought flagged and faltered in tacking, that we are
able to ascertain what advance has been made. Even
here it is true that there is no advance without connection, where the one is precocious and the other dubious.

The advance from general inhospitality to the barren rock is
only from a principle to a detail, or, if you prefer it, from a
rule to an exception—according as you find it in or out of
keeping with the shabbiness of the coast. And as to the
connection, what angle of incidence is that, to which for the
life of us we could not adjust our instruments, without an
interregnum of confusion or suspense between alternative
issues ?   How of all modes of transition should that be the
coryphæus and the nonpareil ?   There are two criteria of
progress in composition—advance in logic, and advance in
information; which may be directly or inversely as each
other.   Meantime it is sufficient that all advance in logic
is directly and not inversely as logical connection.   What
we mean by reason and consequent is the recognition, in
abstract speech, of a universal fact in nature; and to *express*
the relation between them is impossible except by assuming
their duality.   We say accordingly: I strike this match,
and therefore it begins to blaze.   The matter we may know
to be identical; but it is the *form*, by which expression is
bound, both form and aft, with a necessity as eternal as its
inability to fix by any fraction of a second the instant in
which the one phenomenon shoots into the other amidships.
But what become the forms of a material substance, under
various conditions in nature, are just the material for a
formal existence like expression.   Being distinct as forms
of a common fact or substance in the physical world, they
are distinct as separate facts, in the world of expression,
under a common form.   The two stand to each other conversely: advance in the natural sphere being from phase to
phase, in the formal, from ultimatum to ultimatum, and the
nexus in the natural sphere being one of material, in the

other one of form. Hence the nexus in the illustration is absolute, founding on physical identity. And similarly, the advance is absolute, from the one idea to its companion. It would be impossible to gauge any degree of advance, without assuming some standard of connection, by which it might be expounded. And consider simply how fiercely hostile two things must be, which, in spite of so perfect a nexus, are yet distinct. Real connection, therefore, being removed as far from *total* identity as from total difference, it is self-evident, that real advance is as far from total difference as from total identity.

COR.—There is no *prerogative* mode of transition in style, any more than there is a prerogative velocity of descent for a heavy body, falling a hundred feet, over a light one. Each is indispensable for its own special function. Nevertheless as the ponderous body will create more heat when it strikes the earth then the light body, so a series of thoughts, with a single order of interconnection (if such a thing were possible), would be more or less rigorous than another, provided the principle of connection there were uniform also. Most passages therefore, and all of any length, exhibit an average cohesion in their transitions.

24.

The necessity, for composition, of a *duality* of ideas to act in combination is also its limit. The principle of extension in thought has nothing to do with an indefinite series of ideas, except by way of providing the elementary conditions of each. In the middle, or at the end, the series does no more than repeat its experiences at the beginning: it is simply the bridge of which these are the arches. It is not they, there-

fore, that are subdivisions from the series, but the series which
is an accumulation of such integral portions. And in every
case of transposition or transformation of the larger masses, it
is they that regulate the result—not they through any section
or whole, but the section through them.

In the process, which in composition is continually
going forward, of alternate grasping and releasing by the
attention—grasping that it may release, and releasing
that it may grasp—the motion of style is necessarily
modified by the number of ideas that can be received at
the same moment in sufficient force to be co-ordinated.
The process is one taking place with the full consciousness of the writer. But concurrently with this, there may
be a subconscious process, moulding the thought as a
whole into conformity with one dominant idea, not
dispersed through the thoughts separately, but secretly
determining the bias of all. These influence each other
very greatly; it depends, for example, on the rigid connection of its members, that a train of thought completes
its curriculum round a given centre, so as to produce a
symmetrical result; and on the stability of its focus (which
may be complex, but must be distinctly conceived), that a
series of ideas forms a recognisable whole. What, therefore, in theory is the evolution of a determinate conception
through its separate phases, is in practice the setting of these
into mosaic—the conscious formation of successive details
to a totality subconsciously fixed, subconsciously regulative.
That totality, having been reached, may be regarded consciously as a whole; in which event the principle is
reversed, the totality is recognized explicitly, and the
details implicitly. Such a mode of regarding the affect of

a piece of composition is, therefore, the exact converse of
the stylic. Style, being concerned with the process of
movement, has nothing to do with results. In its own way,
it has accounted for every item in the whole composition—
for every slide and pirouette, for every jerk and oscillation
—not a crevice remains for explanation. Any other mode
of explaining the facts must transcend style, and *ex
hypothesi* cannot be stylic; it is simply rhetorical. Now
evidently the same function, which deals with the effect of
the sections of a piece, deals *a fortiori* with the totality of
the piece. And the rhetorical relation of any piece being
that in which it is a universal, and the stylic that in which
it is regarded in its particulars, the same rhetorical function,
which treats of every complete piece in relation to its
sections, treats also of these in relation to their subsections,
and mediately to the individual reticulations of the latter
in style.—Another mode of viewing a passage, quite distinct from either of these, but rhetorical also in its application, is by estimating its general brilliance of connection.
" Most passages, and all of any length, exhibit an average
cohesion in their transitions." But the total estimate in
such a case founds solely on the aggregation of individual
brilliances, separately noted in any review for purposes of
style.—Casually, of course, the last thought of a section
may inosculate as closely with the first of the succeeding
one, as if the latter were simply a continuation of the self-
same idea. Indeed the more closely a writer mediates his
thoughts the one through the other, in relation to the total
idea, there will be the more difficulty in determining where
his new sections begin, apart from some mechanical device
for advertising such a transition. Which artificial device,

K

as we have it now-a-days, is quite inadequate to distinguish
the hierarchies of articulation, of section and subsection;
and is in fact often misleading, because it confounds what
is co-ordinate with what is subordinate.   But a writer has no
business to play fast and loose with the one distinction that
is recognized so sacredly, that viz. between the section and
the proposition.   He may, if he likes, turn a waggon-load
of small paragraphs into one, with a view to keeping the
resources of the paragraph for the grouping of the larger
masses of his thought.   But in that case, he ought to be
the very last person who should wish to distribute one
section into two.   It is very ungenteel to straddle back
against a door-post, one leg in the room, and the other in
the lobby.   Indefeasibly his section is one and continuous,
notwithstanding the mechanical division.   And when a
French novelist writes: "Jacques could not collect his
thoughts—Why?—He was mad,"—in three parallel lines,
we pass it without remark, because it is too furious an
exaggeration to be harmful, or to escape anybody's notice.
On the other hand, when a section opens, for example, with
a " therefore," we take the first conception to be a resultant
of the preceding section as a whole, and not of its last proposition.   If the two sections are specifically unconnected
in their drift, our author should either give a different turn
to the inaugural proposition, or omit it altogether.

Cor.—No writer holds more than one total thought at a time
in relation to any other, whether that be one already completed, or one that suggests itself as the resolution of the
thought under formation.   This number is a constant in all
composition.   Any variation between man and man occurs in
two ways.   In the one instance, it depends upon the rapidity

with which the individual composes. In the other, it depends on the complexity of the conception. Virtually there is
often a plurality of suggestions moving abreast at once, and
threatening to break the critical nexus; and there arises a
counteracting force, not to extend the limit, however, but to
cause the thoughts to travel backwards and adapt themselves
to it. The machinery, by which the attention is thus virtually expanded, and the volume of the thought increased, is
that of Intension.

Section III.   Of Intension.

25.

There are certain relations (such as that of cause and effect),
to which, from their essential coherence, it is indifferent *per se*
whether they shall be expressed in one proposition or in two.
These are of a bivalvular form, that no compression will hide,
and no extension disunite. In the second place, there are
many thoughts which are indivisible, and can only be stated
independently; for example, "The rate of discount varies
with the degree of commercial prosperity." But finally,
there are certain conceptions, which cannot adequately be
expressed, unless their special relation is expressed *within* the
proposition; whose totality is not complete, is not significant,
without a limitation. They resemble the second class of
ideas, in so far as they are formally single; but are unlike, in
so far as they approximate to being substantially dual propositions. And it is in this latter point that they resemble
the first class, while they differ from that by not containing
their two factors in the same exact equilibrium. By way of
illustration, I may say, with reference to the distinction in

point, "This class of marsupial propositions resembles the
first, only in so far as it approximates to a division of substance;" and virtually I have expressed by intension all that
could be expressed by extending the position into a separate
phrase.

If you assert, without its accompanying limitation, the
fact that "all persons holding property exercise the right of
suffrage, except women," you assert what is false. If again
it is expressed thus, "No women have the right of suffrage,"
the fact of the exception is still omitted; and there is an
appeal made to the imagination of the reader to supply
what is involved, viz. that every one else has it. Which
appeal is either premature or gratuitous; since if the reader
does not know anything about the fact, he will not gain it
from such a bare statement; and if he does know it, and all
that remains is to insist upon it oratorically, you forego the
chance of parading it with that special emphasis which the
discarded relation expressly secures. The thought thus
being coaxed into a simple proposition, there flies into the
wilderness the very point of having a complex formula.
Nor, if you express it in a double proposition, will you
whistle your hawk back from the wilderness. For express
yourself thus: "All men have the right of suffrage—but
women have it not,"—and it will be evident that you have
simply adjusted the two facts *as particular to particular*.
And meantime, the logical principle, which is radiantly acknowledged in the proposition as it stood originally, and of
whose organic force this is the complete abnegation, is that
of the *universal to the particular*. This form of statement
has its own use in the economy of transitions. By which I
mean to infer, that it only comes into collision with other

forms, upon a question arising of differential propriety. And on the other hand, I infer that it is liable to be drawn into spurious comparisons, by the perversions or neglect of its own principle—by a writer's treating, as if it were subordinate, what is of cardinal import, and using the machinery of inter-propositional connection for what is strictly intra-propositionaL

COR.—Even in a mere literary fashion, the principle of subordination is of use to preserve the thought against diverging from the main issue. Were there no such resource, co-ordinate and subordinate relations would be confounded together. And consequently, it relieves the pressure that otherwise must overtake the function of simple transition; especially where the new limb of the proposition expresses no specific limitation, but a casual addition to the thought. Thus in reporting on the fact that Major X. (who had recently returned to this country from the East) was about to publish a volume of travels, the parenthetical clause is admissible, which would have been out of place as an independent truth between that fact and the disjunct fact, that the Major's experiences had extended over a great number of years. Indeed it would be admissible even as a separate fact (e.g. Major X. is about to publish a volume of travels—He has lately returned from the East) provided something else be put in the stead of the third sentence; upon the principle that you may ask a person to dine with yourself and a confidential friend, whom you would not ask to dine with your friends promiscuously. Hence another value of the process of subordination, as an alternative mode of *varying* the form of transition —the first form in which the illustration stood being a variety of the last—apart from the resource of making the clausal

addition in any thought the specific link of connection between
it and the next.

26.

Some machinery, then, must plainly be devised for incorporat-
ing into a proposition, without offence, collateral or supplementary statements, that, if explicated in full, would disturb
the principle of progression, and for recognising as subordinate
those which perforce had incorporated themselves in the
uncompleted thinking. Statements there are, which may be
preserved as additions, without encumbering the conception,
and be identified with it, without abating their significance.
The abuses of the process are threefold. (1) The apparatus of
subordination may be applied to an idea which ought to be
explicated in full further on, perhaps with a whole flourish
of pendants of its own. (2) There is the case in which a
suggestion is introduced, hanging merely by some happy-go-
lucky connection, or quite irrelevant. Greater laxity is allowed
to a subordinating principle than to one of co-ordination. But
whatever tells in the case of the one tells in a corresponding
degree in the case of the other. (3) There is a chance of the
principle of the minor clause being indefinitely repeated.
This is the chief danger. And it is this which makes any
exaggeration of the others so much to be dreaded: in the
second instance, it would be to add irrelevance to irrelevance,
impertinence within impertinence. The abstract ideal and
the practical, with regard to the statement of relative truth,
have no such intimate connection with each other, as in the case
of the integral statement of truth absolute. A single statement of truth in the abstract, that should include in it implicitly every other truth, would be essentially compendious.

A single statement of truth in its subordination—in its processions and divisions, its oppositions and concessions—would include every express relation of every truth to every other: it would be essentially pancyclopædic. The attention could not yield to the strain for a moment; it would not even try to prefigure the eternally advancing, eternally receding conclusion. It bends, therefore, to the same limitations in intension as in extension. Being flushed from the primary thought, and overflowing, it returns to fill the *lacuna* which it had anticipated in the thought that succeeds; its practical limit not interfering with, but specifically enhancing any purposes of literary propriety—of perspicuity, or economy, or elegance.

The medium for the distribution of the energy of subordination in thought is again the faculty of attention. It is not attention, however (any more than in the preceding case), in the sense of that which is exhausted during the evolution of thought, and every exertion of which involves a separate decrement in the stock of available energy. For so far as exhaustion goes, it does not matter to the reader whether that is effected by fifty curt propositions, or by twenty voluminous ones. Fatigue is no independent criterion, therefore; and even as a symptom it is inconstant and precarious. Moreover, its degree, when it does move in an appreciable ratio, is itself otherwise predetermined, viz. by the intellectual conditions for apprehending rapidly the bearing of a new thought, and for sustaining it without impatience through its development to its technical sublation in the thought which succeeds. It is not attention in its length that is meant, but in its breadth—the capacity for holding a number of conceptions simultaneously, so as to form a unity, varying in complexity according to the clearness with which these may be combined.

Cor.—The principle of certain writings conducted apparently in defiance of this limit is really exoteric. The structure of law documents is often according to a coarse and very different method. The various clauses, instead of being embraced in a unity of consciousness, are held together in the *memory*. This, psychologically, is the distinction; the unity in transition being often merely arbitrary and precarious.

27.

Every proposition must be either simple or complex. If simple, however, it may be so by having rejected the chance of forming a member of a complex proposition; and if complex, it may be so by refusing to have its members scattered into separate propositions. The permutations, according to which the several limbs of an original complex thought may be arranged, are very numerous. Only each of these, as ultimately placed, is still one of the two alternative forms, either a simple thought or a compound, and is alternatively that which it is, by having refused to incarnate itself under the correlative form. This is the simple case, in which the reader sees all the apparent alternatives spread out on the page before him at once. Nor is it worth while inquiring particularly into the hidden alternatives;—what might have happened, viz. in the way of *suppression*, before the thought was permitted to stand as it is. All that moves agreeably to the same principles. So in the case of revision: if a new thought is to be admitted, it must be either as an integral fact, or as a fact in affiliation with some other fact (must be a leading fact, or a secondary, or an offshoot again from that), whether it be

as a total increment, or as a substitute for some other fact
that has been suppressed. Any alteration must take effect
either (1) by way of addition, or (2) by way of retractation,
or (3) of both combined, the new fact being promoted *vice* the
previous fact superannuated.—Even here of course there is a
mode of keeping the thought in life, viz. the appendix, or
note; which may radiate from the original suggestion of the
text at various angles, and with varying degrees of importance.
Only its scope is limited; otherwise, upon the same principle,
a succession of notes, taking off from each other, might be
continued *ad infinitum.* And besides, exhibiting in itself the
same principles of composition which govern the primary
text, the note has no special value as illustrating how these
work.—So far there is nothing to alter—to multiply or
diminish—the forms under which the result must appear.
But these processes throw a very searching light upon the
secret rationale of variety in composition, and a very significant one upon the reciprocal relations of transition and
subordination. Interpose a thought between two complex
thoughts, and possibly you will attract the allegiance of their
near members to itself, transmuting what is left into a simple
transitional phase from an ultra-transitional. Eliminate a
proposition, and the thoughts, between which it has stood,
may coalesce. Each resultant form, however, will still arise,
just by rejecting the form in which it would not be what it is.
This simply is the differential principle in Quantity, which
by the side of Quality is too apt to appear flaccid and
meagre, and which these external modes of variation tend
vastly to enhance and expound, by illustrating the organic
nature of transitional connection.

To say that one thought may influence the form of

another standing in connection with it, is to say nothing.
It gives no clue to the degree or the kind of variation which
may be involved. For, transition being known to be the
most important matter in composing, we should each of us
naturally incline to look upon any modification arising
within that as very trifling. And as a rule it is so: so long
as the change descends upon the subordinate clauses it is
inconsiderable. "An immense majority of the Roman
people never lighted a candle, unless sometimes in the
early dawn. And this custom was the custom of all
nations that lived round the Mediterranean." Let the final
clause be eliminated from the first proposition, and it will
make no difference to the connection of the two sentences;
since the reference in the latter is to the rule, not to the
exception. Upon the same principle, the corresponding
clause in the text of this sentence, which I have suppressed,
ought to be superfluous. "The daylight furnished gratis
was certainly undeniable in its quality. . . . Seneca even in
his own luxurious period called those men by ugly names
who lived chiefly by candle-light." Yet no; there is a
hiatus. For why "ugly"? Because the men were too
ugly themselves to come abroad in the day-time, or because
they were luxurious, or perhaps because they were candle-
making, which being such a public disgrace, itself required
to be prosecuted by artificial (to wit candle) light? For no
such reason, but for one more obvious, yet still puzzling,
because one of *several* more or less obvious reasons,—which
is supplied by the intercalated phrase, "quite sufficient for
all purposes that were *honest*." The difference of variation
in the first instance is at its minimum, in the other at its
maximum, the complex proposition in the one case being

virtually a simple thought, in the other virtually a dual.

Now let both clauses, instead of being suppressed, undergo the other change, that of elevation into an independent thought. Immediately the values are reversed. The subordinate member of the first instance is seen to be incompatible with the seriousness of the transition that is made to rest upon it; while, in the other case, the alteration makes very little real difference. The degree of variation is now at its maximum in the first case, and at its minimum in the second.

The difference of variation, therefore, exists at a maximum or a minimum, according as in each case the alternative orders of circumstance take effect; the same condition in either producing the opposite result to that which it produces in the other, and the same ratio of effect being produced in the one as is produced by the opposite condition in the other. The general principle, however, is (1) that of intermodification (and not of suppression), and (2) that of a maximum change under such intermodification—a subordinate clause being raised to the rank of a separate proposition. Now if this is the ordinary case, it will not do simply to say that one proposition affects the form of its neighbour; which implies that the change is quite inconsiderable. Especially the degree of the variation requires to be specified, when it is the exception to the second rule that is to be taken into account, and the change is a minimum, the subordinate clause being virtually a co-ordinate already, and benefiting little by its promotion. Still more peremptorily does the *nature* of the variation require to be adjusted, when (the first law being violated) it

is a suppression, and not a mere alteration of form; since
that suppression brings this last exceptional minimum
change of the subordinate clause to the normal maximum,
and the first normal maximum change to an exceptional
minimum. It would be utterly vain, therefore, to look in
the mere form of a proposition for a clue to its transitional
value; and just for this reason, that there are only the two
forms—compromise between them there is none. No more
palpable distinction of form can exist between a pot with a
handle and a pot without. And it is all the more readily
assumed, that the substantial value of each is uniformly the
same; while none could be more equivocal. Meantime, the
possible modification that may be produced by one proposition upon another is modification enough; in the first
instance the sentence following the clause "unless perhaps," etc., determines that that clause, if introduced, shall
not be co-ordinate with it, but must be subordinate to
the preceding thought; and in the second instance,
the subordinate clause determines that the succeeding
proposition shall not supplant it, but must stand
apart.

COR.—The interaction of the two fundamental processes in
composition is the ground not more of certain average effects
in style, than of certain broad differences. No man writes
without using both; but they may be used in different proportions, so as to distinguish even diverse nationalities. And
a tariff might even be fixed for certain artificial stimulants,
according to the results of their physiological action upon the
several processes of composition. The effect of wine, for
example, appears to be that of inducing a more brusque and
discontinuous mode of writing, and to discourage a more

elaborate style of movement, the tendency to which is doubtless exaggerated by opium.

More immediately, however, the power of literary condensation depends upon a knowledge of the manner in which
these processes mutually affect each other. Most people seem
to think that the way to condense is by suppression. Let a
writer run his pen through a sentence here, and a clause there,
and he does all that is required. Especially, it would be said,
let the carnage descend most heavily on the clauses. Now
really it is not the derivative and parenthetical clauses that
harbour diffuseness, but the garrulous or querulous iteration
of the same truth in successive propositions. Nevertheless
let the clauses be thinned out. And let your redundant main
propositions be dismissed at the same time. But now, where
many people imagine the work of compression to be over, the
important part of it is just beginning. Only instead of com-
mencing with the secondary clauses, we commence with the
primary; and instead of lessening the number of subordina-
tions, we increase them, by making the co-ordinate propositions
coalesce, and subordinating one to the other.

All practical instruction in the art of composition flows
naturally out of these principles. As for mechanical criteria,
they are of no use. Direct the tyro to write in long sentences,
or in short sentences, and you tell him nothing. There may
be more difference between two short propositions than
between a short and a long. A thought, for example, with a
significant exception attached to it, and that turns back upon
itself at a very acute angle, may make more demand upon the
attention than one which carries the leading idea through a
whole series of antistrophes. To talk of brevity, with a distinction like that concealed under it, is to give no hint of the

real case, to a pupil who measures results by the square foot,
and possibly to encourage a vicious style of writing, by leaving him to suppose that one curt proposition is as good as
another.   Now a *staccato* movement of thought is not merely
one of the most offensive, but specifically the most unpromis-
ing of all the modes of composition.   In its own degree the
most lively, it is in continuity the most monotonous.   And
in a higher sense it is vicious, because it generates irreflec-
tion ; which is a vice, just in proportion as the majority of
truths are relative.   The most effective mode of statement is
that of a truth in its relations.   Accordingly your true rhetorician aims chiefly at such results, not because they are the
most elaborate, or the most uncommon, but simply because
they are the most telling.   Fantasias he can spin by the
hour, when the mood impels him, but his preference is for a
severer brilliance.   He trusts, for his music, to precision, and,
for his artistry, to the rigour of his proportions.   It is here
that your ordinary rhetorician discovers another weakness.
Having finished his tale of short propositions, he thinks to
take it out in long boa-constrictor periods, with a good deal
less of the fantasia, and a very great deal more of the spin-
ning.   For as there are effects of the turkey-cock order, so
there is a class of people who go about gobbling upon a very
limited amount of provocation—afflicted with a sort of sodden
enthusiasm, borrowed from the memory of platform excite-
ment, or from imitations of such memories.   Now the undula-
tion and the swoop, the strenuousness and the ease, which
ought to mark the rhetorical wave are in general all very well
—for the sea.   Nevertheless, if his foam does not look like
lather, nor the movement of the water betray a surreptitious
besom—so long as his waves slop and lunge, and rally for an

instant before the fall, and flounce over in mist and thunder
—a man does well. And unquestionably, even a pretentious
effect is not nearly so bad as the practice of involution, when
carried to an excess. For that there is no defence. Nevertheless, it may arise sometimes from an exceptional power of
manœuvring complicated truth, and not from slovenliness,
which in literature is often a species of locomotor ataxy.
And for that reason it is not to be regarded as something
very heinous by the side of the tendency to extreme brevity.
Of the two it is that which promises best for amendment;
since the positive tendency in it is more easily checked than
the partial tendency in the other is likely to be developed.
This is true, however, only so long as each is regarded specifically as a tendency : as an intermittent effect the subsultory
order of proposition is of great use, but the other never. And
this is the rationale of the value of the short proposition
generally, as opposed to the long, either *per se* being indifferent
—viz. that as an effect alternating with a proposition of
moderate length, it is better than the other; it behaves better
in combination. But it is not the normal proposition; that
is calculated from the medium, not from either extreme.
The proposition of medium length is the constant, and is
relieved most effectively by the one variable which is *not* the
most cumbrous; upon the same principle that, in waltzing,
it is better for a man—he being the active or determining
force—to have a partner shorter than himself, rather than
one who is proportionately taller.

39 PATERNOSTER ROW, E.C.
LONDON, *November* 1874.

GENERAL LIST OF WORKS

PUBLISHED BY

MESSRS. LONGMANS, GREEN, AND CO.

	PAGE		PAGE
ARTS, MANUFACTURES, &c.	25	MENTAL & POLITICAL PHILOSOPHY	8
ASTRONOMY & METEOROLOGY	17	MISCELLANEOUS & CRITICAL WORKS	12
BIOGRAPHICAL WORKS	6	NATURAL HISTORY & PHYSICAL	
CHEMISTRY & PHYSIOLOGY	23	SCIENCE	18
DICTIONARIES & other BOOKS of		POETRY & the DRAMA	35
REFERENCE	14	RELIGIOUS & MORAL WORKS	28
FINE ARTS & ILLUSTRATED EDI-		RURAL SPORTS, HORSE & CATTLE	
TIONS	24	MANAGEMENT, &c.	36
HISTORY, POLITICS, HISTORICAL		TRAVELS, VOYAGES, &c.	32
MEMOIRS, &c.	1	WORKS of FICTION	34
INDEX	41 to 44	WORKS of UTILITY & GENERAL	
KNOWLEDGE for the YOUNG	40	INFORMATION	38

HISTORY, POLITICS, HISTORICAL MEMOIRS, &c.

Journal of the Reigns of King George IV. and King William IV.

By the late Charles C. F. Greville, Esq. Clerk of the Council to those Sovereigns. Edited by Henry Reeve, Registrar of the Privy Council.

3 *vols.* 8vo. *price* 36s.

The Life of Napoleon III. derived from State Records, Unpublished Family Correspondence, and Personal Testimony.

By Blanchard Jerrold.

Four Vols. 8vo. with Portraits from the Originals in possession of the Imperial Family, and Facsimiles of Letters of Napoleon I. Napoleon III. Queen Hortense, &c. VOL. I. *price* 18s.

*** *Vol. II. will be published in the Autumn, and Vols. III. and IV. completing the work, in the Spring of* 1875.

A

Recollections and Suggestions of Public Life, 1813–1873.
By *John Earl Russell.*
1 vol. 8vo.   [*Nearly ready.*

Introductory Lectures on Modern History delivered in Lent Term 1842 ; with the Inaugural Lecture delivered in December 1841.
By the late Rev. Thomas Arnold, D.D.
8vo. price 7s. 6d.

Essays on the English Government and Constitution from the Reign of Henry VII. to the Present Time.
By *John Earl Russell.*
Fcp. 8vo. 3s. 6d.

On Parliamentary Government in England: its Origin, Development, and Practical Operation.
By *Alpheus Todd.*
2 vols. 8vo. £1. 17s.

The Constitutional History of England since the Accession of George III. 1760–1870.
By *Sir Thomas Erskine May, K.C.B.*
Fourth Edition. 3 vols. crown 8vo. 18s.

Democracy in Europe; a History.
By *Sir Thomas Erskine May, K.C.B.*
2 vols. 8vo.   [*In preparation.*

The History of England from the Fall of Wolsey to the Defeat of the Spanish Armada.
By *J. A. Froude, M.A.*
CABINET EDITION, 12 vols. cr. 8vo. £3. 12s.
LIBRARY EDITION, 12 vols. 8vo. £8. 18s.

The English in Ireland in the Eighteenth Century.
By *J. A. Froude, M.A.*
3 vols. 8vo. £2. 8s.

Estimates of the English Kings from William the Conqueror to George III.
By *J. L. Sanford.*
Crown 8vo. 12s. 6d.

The History of England from the Accession of James II.
By *Lord Macaulay.*
STUDENT'S EDITION, 2 vols. cr. 8vo. 12s.
PEOPLE'S EDITION, 4 vols. cr. 8vo. 16s.
CABINET EDITION, 8 vols. post 8vo. 48s.
LIBRARY EDITION, 5 vols. 8vo. £4.

Critical and Historical Essays contributed to the Edinburgh Review.
By the Right Hon. Lord Macaulay.
Cheap Edition, authorised and complete, crown 8vo. 3s. 6d.
STUDENT'S EDITION, crown 8vo. 6s.
PEOPLE'S EDITION, 2 vols. crown 8vo. 8s.
CABINET EDITION, 4 vols. 24s.
LIBRARY EDITION, 3 vols. 8vo. 36s.

Lord Macaulay's Works.
Complete and uniform Library Edition.
Edited by his Sister, Lady Trevelyan.
8 vols. 8vo. with Portrait, £5. 5s.

Lectures on the History of England from the Earliest Times to the Death of King Edward II.
By W. Longman, F.A.S.
Maps and Illustrations. 8vo. 15s.

The History of the Life and Times of Edward III.
By W. Longman, F.A.S.
With 9 Maps, 8 Plates, and 16 Woodcuts. 2 vols. 8vo. 28s.

History of England under the Duke of Buckingham and Charles the First, 1624–1628.
By S. Rawson Gardiner, late Student of Ch. Ch.
2 vols. 8vo.   [In the press.

History of Civilization in England and France, Spain and Scotland.
By Henry Thomas Buckle.
3 vols. crown 8vo. 24s.

A Student's Manual of the History of India from the Earliest Period to the Present.
By Col. Meadows Taylor, M.R.A.S.
Second Thousand. Cr. 8vo. Maps, 7s. 6d.

The French Revolution and First Empire; an Historical Sketch.
By W. O'Connor Morris, sometime Scholar of Oriel College, Oxford.
With 2 Maps. Post 8vo. 7s. 6d.

The History of India from the Earliest Period to the close of Lord Dalhousie's Administration.
By John Clark Marshman.
3 vols. crown 8vo. 22s. 6d.

Indian Polity; a View of the System of Administration in India. .
By Lieut.-Colonel George Chesney.
Second Edition, revised, with Map. 8vo. 21s.

Waterloo Lectures; a Study of the Campaign of 1815.
By Colonel Charles C. Chesney, R.E.
Third Edition. 8vo. with Map, 10s. 6d.

Essays in Modern Military Biography.
By Colonel Charles C. Chesney, R.E.
8vo. 12s. 6d.

The Imperial and Colonial Constitutions of the Britannic Empire, including Indian Institutions.
By Sir E. Creasy, M.A.
With 6 Maps. 8vo. 15s.

The Oxford Reformers— John Colet, Erasmus, and Thomas More; being a History of their Fellow-Work.
By Frederic Seebohm.
Second Edition. 8vo. 14s.

The History of Persia and its present Political Situation; with Abstracts of all Treaties and Conventions between Persia and England.
By Clements R. Markham, C.B. F.R.S.
8vo. with Map, 21s.

The Mythology of the Aryan Nations.
By Geo. W. Cox, M.A. late Scholar of Trinity College, Oxford.
2 vols. 8vo. 28s.

A History of Greece.
By the Rev. Geo. W. Cox, M.A. late Scholar of Trinity College, Oxford.
Vols. I. and II. 8vo. Maps, 36s.

The History of Greece.
By C. Thirlwall, D.D. late Bp. of St. David's.
8 vols. fcp. 8vo. 28s.

The Tale of the Great Persian War, from the Histories of Herodotus.
By Rev. G. W. Cox, M.A.
Fcp. 8vo. 3s. 6d.

The History of the Peloponnesian War, by Thucydides.
Translated by Richd. Crawley, Fellow of Worcester College, Oxford.
8vo. 21s.

Greek History from Themistocles to Alexander, in a Series of Lives from Plutarch.
Revised and arranged by A. H. Clough.
Fcp. 8vo. Woodcuts, 6s.

History of the Romans under the Empire.
By the Very Rev. Charles Merivale, D.C.L. Dean of Ely.
8 vols. post 8vo. 48s.

The Fall of the Roman Republic; a Short History of the Last Century of the Commonwealth.
By Dean Merivale, D.C.L.
12mo. 7s. 6d.

The Sixth Oriental Monarchy; or the Geography, History, and Antiquities of Parthia. Collected and Illustrated from Ancient and Modern sources.
By Geo. Rawlinson, M.A.
With Maps and Illustrations. 8vo. 16s.

The Seventh Great Oriental Monarchy; or, a History of the Sassanians: with Notices Geographical and Antiquarian.
By Geo. Rawlinson, M.A.
8vo. with Maps and Illustrations.
[In the press.

Encyclopædia of Chronology, Historical and Biographical; comprising the Dates of all the Great Events of History, including Treaties, Alliances, Wars, Battles, &c. Incidents in the Lives of Eminent Men, Scientific and Geographical Discoveries, Mechanical Inventions, and Social, Domestic, and Economical Improvements.
By B. B. Woodward, B.A. and W. L. R. Cates.
8vo. 42s.

The History of Rome.
By Wilhelm Ihne.
Vols. I. and II. 8vo. 30s. Vols. III. and IV. in preparation.

History of European Morals from Augustus to Charlemagne.
By W. E. H. Lecky, M.A.
2 vols. 8vo. 28s.

History of the Rise and Influence of the Spirit of Rationalism in Europe.
By W. E. H. Lecky, M.A.
Cabinet Edition, 2 vols. crown 8vo. 16s.

History of the Early Church from the First Preaching of the Gospel to the Council of Nicæa, A.D. 325.
By Miss E. M. Sewell.
Fcp. 8vo. 4s. 6d.

Introduction to the Science of Religion: Four Lectures delivered at the Royal Institution; with two Essays on False Analogies and the Philosophy of Mythology.
By F. Max Müller, M.A.
Crown 8vo. 10s. 6d.

The Stoics, Epicureans, and Sceptics.
Translated from the German of Dr. E. Zeller, by Oswald J. Reichel, M.A.
Crown 8vo. 14s.

Socrates and the Socratic Schools.
Translated from the German of Dr. E. Zeller, by the Rev. O. J. Reichel, M.A.
Crown 8vo. 8s. 6d.

The History of Philosophy, from Thales to Comte.
By George Henry Lewes.
Fourth Edition, 2 vols. 8vo. 32s.

Sketch of the History of the Church of England to the Revolution of 1688.
By the Right Rev. T. V. Short, D.D. Bishop of St. Asaph.
Eighth Edition. Crown 8vo. 7s. 6d.

The Historical Geography of Europe.
By E. A. Freeman, D.C.L.
8vo. Maps. [In the press.

Essays on the History of the Christian Religion.
By *John Earl Russell.*
Fcp. 8vo. 3s. 6d.

History of the Reformation in Europe in the Time of Calvin.
By the Rev. *J. H. Merle D'Aubigné, D.D.*
Vols. I. to V. 8vo. £3. 12s. Vols. VI. & VII. completion, [In the press.

The Student's Manual of Ancient History: containing the Political History, Geographical Position, and Social State of the Principal Nations of Antiquity.
By *W. Cooke Taylor, LL.D.*
Crown 8vo. 7s. 6d.

The Student's Manual of Modern History: containing the Rise and Progress of the Principal European Nations, their Political History, and the Changes in their Social Condition.
By *W. Cooke Taylor, LL.D.*
Crown 8vo. 7s. 6d.

The Era of the Protestant Revolution.
By *F. Seebohm, Author of 'The Oxford Reformers.'*
With 4 Maps and 12 Diagrams. Fcp. 8vo. 2s. 6d.

The Crusades.
By the Rev. *G. W. Cox, M.A.*
Fcp. 8vo. with Map, 2s. 6d.

The Thirty Years' War, 1618–1648.
By *Samuel Rawson Gardiner.*
Fcp. 8vo. with Maps, 2s. 6d.

The Houses of Lancaster and York; with the Conquest and Loss of France.
By *James Gairdner.*
Fcp. 8vo. with Map, 2s. 6d.

Edward the Third.
By the Rev. *W. Warburton, M.A.*
Fcp. 8vo. with Maps, 2s. 6d.

BIOGRAPHICAL WORKS.

Autobiography.
By *John Stuart Mill.*
8vo. 7s. 6d.

Life and Correspondence of Richard Whately, D.D. late Archbishop of Dublin.
By *E. Jane Whately.*
New Edition in 1 vol. Crown 8vo. [In the press.

Life and Letters of Gilbert Elliot, First Earl of Minto, from 1751 to 1806, when his Public Life in Europe was closed by his Appointment to the Vice-Royalty of India.
Edited by the Countess of Minto.
3 vols. post 8vo. 31s. 6d.

Memoir of Thomas First
Lord Denman, formerly
Lord Chief Justice of
England.
By Sir Joseph Arnould,
B.A. K.B.
With two Portraits. 2 vols. 8vo. 32s.

The Life of Lloyd First
Lord Kenyon.
By Hon. G. T. Kenyon,
M.A.
With Portraits. 8vo. 14s.

Recollections of Past
Life.
By Sir Henry Holland,
Bart. M.D. F.R.S.
Third Edition. Post 8vo. 10s. 6d.

Isaac Casaubon, 1559-
1614.
By Mark Pattison, Rector
of Lincoln College, Oxford.
8vo.   *[In the press.*

Life of Alexander von
Humboldt.
Edited by Karl Bruhns,
and translated by Jane
and Caroline Lassell.
With 3 Portraits. 2 vols. 8vo. 36s.

Biographical and Criti-
cal Essays, reprinted from
Reviews, with Additions
and Corrections.
By A. Hayward, Q.C.
*Second Series, 2 vols. 8vo. 28s. Third
Series, 1 vol. 8vo. 14s.*

The Life of Isambard
Kingdom Brunel, Civil
Engineer.
By I. Brunel, B.C.L.
*With Portrait, Plates, and Woodcuts.
8vo. 21s.*

Lord George Bentinck;
a Political Biography.
By the Right Hon. B.
Disraeli, M.P.
Eighth Edition. Crown 8vo. 6s.

Memoir of George Ed-
ward Lynch Cotton, D.D.
Bishop of Calcutta; with
Selections from his Jour-
nals and Correspondence.
Edited by Mrs. Cotton.
Second Edition. Crown 8vo. 7s. 6d.

The Life and Letters of
the Rev. Sydney Smith.
Edited by his Daughter,
Lady Holland, and
Mrs. Austin.
Crown 8vo. 2s. 6d. sewed; 3s. 6d. cloth.

Essays in Ecclesiastical
Biography.
By the Right Hon. Sir J.
Stephen, LL.D.
Cabinet Edition. Crown 8vo. 7s. 6d.

Leaders of Public Opi-
nion in Ireland; Swift,
Flood, Grattan, O'Connell.
By W. E. H. Lecky, M.A.
Crown 8vo. 7s. 6d.

Life of the Duke of Wellington.
By the Rev. G. R. Gleig, M.A.

Popular Edition, Crown 8vo. with Portrait, 5s.

Felix Mendelssohn's
Letters from Italy and Switzerland, and Letters from 1833 to 1847.
Translated by Lady Wallace.

With Portrait. 2 vols. crown 8vo. 5s. each.

The Rise of Great Families; other Essays and Stories.
By Sir Bernard Burke, C.B. LL.D.

Crown 8vo. 12s. 6d.

Dictionary of General Biography; containing Concise Memoirs and Notices of the most Eminent Persons of all Countries, from the Earliest Ages to the Present Time.
Edited by W. L. R. Cates.

8vo. 21s.

Memoirs of Sir Henry Havelock, K.C.B.
By John Clark Marshman.

People's Edition. Crown 8vo. 3s. 6d.

Vicissitudes of Families.
By Sir Bernard Burke, C.B.

New Edition. 2 vols. crown 8vo. 21s.

MENTAL and POLITICAL PHILOSOPHY.

The System of Positive Polity, or Treatise upon Sociology, of Auguste Comte, Author of the System of Positive Philosophy.

Translated from the Paris Edition of 1851-1854, and furnished with Analytical Tables of Contents.

[In preparation.

In Four Volumes, 8vo. to be published separately, and each forming in some degree an independent Treatise:—

Vol. I. The General View of Positive Polity and its Philosophical Basis. Translated by J. H. Bridges, M.B. formerly Fellow Oriel College, Oxford.

Vol. II. The Social Statics, or the Ab-
stract Laws of Human Order. Translated by Frederic Harrison, M.A. of Lincoln's Inn.

Vol. III. The Social Dynamics, or the General Laws of Human Progress (the Philosophy of History). Translated by E. S. Beesly, M.A. Professor of History in University College, London.

Vol. IV. The Ideal of the Future of Mankind. Translated by Richard Congreve, M.D. formerly Fellow and Tutor of Wadham College, Oxford.

Political Problems, Reprinted chiefly from the Fortnightly Review, revised, and with New Essays.
By Frederick Harrison, of Lincoln's Inn.

1 vol. 8vo. [In the press.

Essays Critical & Narrative, partly original and partly reprinted from Reviews.
By W. Forsyth, Q.C. M.P.
8vo. 16s.

Essays, Political, Social, and Religions.
By Richd. Congreve, M.A.
8vo. 18s.

Essays on Freethinking and Plainspeaking.
By Leslie Stephen.
Crown 8vo. 10s. 6d.

Essays, Critical and Biographical, contributed to the Edinburgh Review.
By Henry Rogers.
New Edition. 2 vols. crown 8vo. 12s.

Essays on some Theological Controversies of the Time, contributed chiefly to the Edinburgh Review.
By the same Author.
New Edition. Crown 8vo. 6s.

Democracy in America.
By Alexis de Tocqueville.
Translated by Henry Reeve, C.B. D.C.L. Corresponding Member of the Institute of France.
New Edition. 2 vols. post 8vo. [In the press.

On Representative Government.
By John Stuart Mill.
Fourth Edition, crown 8vo. 2s.

On Liberty.
By John Stuart Mill.
Post 8vo. 7s. 6d. crown 8vo. 1s. 4d.

Principles of Political Economy.
By John Stuart Mill.
2 vols. 8vo. 30s. or 1 vol. crown 8vo. 5s.

Essays on some Unsettled Questions of Political Economy.
By John Stuart Mill.
Second Edition. 8vo. 6s. 6d.

Utilitarianism.
By John Stuart Mill.
Fourth Edition. 8vo. 5s.

A System of Logic, Ratiocinative and Inductive. By John Stuart Mill.
Eighth Edition. 2 vols. 8vo. 25s.

Examination of Sir William Hamilton's Philosophy, and of the principal Philosophical Questions discussed in his Writings.
By John Stuart Mill.
Fourth Edition. 8vo. 16s.

The Subjection of Women.
By John Stuart Mill.
New Edition. Post 8vo. 5s.

Dissertations and Discussions.
By John Stuart Mill.
Second Edition. 3 vols. 8vo. 36s.

B

*Analysis of the Pheno-
mena of the Human Mind.
By James Mill. New
Edition, with Notes,
Illustrative and Critical.*
2 vols. 8vo. 28s.

*A Systematic View of
the Science of Jurispru-
dence.
By Sheldon Amos, M.A.*
8vo. 18s.

*A Primer of the English
Constitution and Govern-
ment.
By Sheldon Amos, M.A.*
New Edition, revised. Post 8vo.
[In the press.

*Principles of Economical
Philosophy.
By H. D. Macleod, M.A.
Barrister-at-Law.*
Second Edition, in 2 vols. Vol. I. 8vo. 15s.

*The Institutes of Jus-
tinian; with English In-
troduction, Translation,
and Notes.
By T. C. Sandars, M.A.*
Sixth Edition. 8vo. 18s.

*Lord Bacon's Works,
Collected and Edited by R.
L. Ellis, M.A. J. Sped-
ding, M.A. and D. D.
Heath.*
New and Cheaper Edition. 7 vols. 8vo.
£3 13s. 6d.

*Letters and Life of
Francis Bacon, including
all his Occasional Works.
Collected and edited, with
a Commentary, by J.
Spedding.*
7 vols. 8vo. £4 4s.

*The Nicomachean Ethics
of Aristotle. Newly translated into English.
By R. Williams, B.A.*
8vo. 12s.

*The Politics of Aristotle;
Greek Text, with English
Notes.
By Richard Congreve, M.A.*
New Edition, revised. 8vo. 18s.

*The Ethics of Aristotle;
with Essays and Notes.
By Sir A. Grant, Bart.
M.A. LL.D.*
Third Edition, revised and partly re-written.
[In the press.

*Bacon's Essays, with
Annotations.
By R. Whately, D.D.*
New Edition. 8vo. 10s. 6d.

*Elements of Logic.
By R. Whately, D.D.*
New Edition. 8vo. 10s. 6d. cr. 8vo. 4s. 6d.

*Elements of Rhetoric.
By R. Whately, D.D.*
New Edition. 8vo. 10s. 6d. cr. 8vo. 4s. 6d.

*An Outline of the Neces-
sary Laws of Thought: a
Treatise on Pure and
Applied Logic.*
By the Most Rev. W.
Thomson, D.D. Arch-
bishop of York.
Ninth Thousand. Crown 8vo. 5s. 6d.

*An Introduction to Men-
tal Philosophy, on the Inductive Method.*
By J. D. Morell, LL.D.
8vo. 12s.

*Elements of Psychology,
containing the Analysis of
the Intellectual Powers.*
By J. D. Morell, LL.D.
Post 8vo. 7s. 6d.

*The Secret of Hegel:
being the Hegelian System
in Origin, Principle, Form,
and Matter.*
By J. H. Stirling, LL.D.
2 vols. 8vo. 28s.

*Sir William Hamilton;
being the Philosophy of
Perception: an Analysis.*
By J. H. Stirling, LL.D.
8vo. 5s.

*The Philosophy of Ne-
cessity; or, Natural Law
as applicable to Mental,
Moral, and Social Science.*
By Charles Bray.
Second Edition. 8vo. 9s.

*Ueberweg's System of
Logic, and History of
Logical Doctrines.*
Translated, with Notes and
Appendices, by T. M.
Lindsay, M.A. F.R.S.E.
8vo. 16s.

*The Senses and the
Intellect.*
By A. Bain, LL.D. Prof.
of Logic, Univ. Aberdeen.
8vo. 15s.

*Mental and Moral
Science; a Compendium of
Psychology and Ethics.*
By A. Bain, LL.D.
Third Edition. Crown 8vo. 10s. 6d. Or
separately: Part I. Mental Science, 6s. 6d.
Part II. Moral Science, 4s. 6d.

*Hume's Treatise on Hu-
man Nature.*
Edited, with Notes, &c. by
T. H. Green, M.A. and
the Rev. T. H. Grose,
M.A.
2 vols. 8vo. 28s.

*Hume's Essays Moral,
Political, and Literary.*
By the same Editors.
2 vols. 8vo. 28s.

. The above form a complete and uniform
Edition of HUME's Philosophical
Works.

MISCELLANEOUS & CRITICAL WORKS.

Miscellaneous and Post-humous Works of the late Henry Thomas Buckle. Edited, with a Biographical Notice, by Helen Taylor.
3 vols. 8vo. £2 12s. 6d.

Short Studies on Great Subjects. By J. A. Froude, M.A. formerly Fellow of Exeter College, Oxford.
2 vols. crown 8vo. 12s.

Lord Macaulay's Miscellaneous Writings.
LIBRARY EDITION, 2 vols. 8vo. Portrait, 21s.
PEOPLE'S EDITION, 1 vol. cr. 8vo. 4s. 6d.

Lord Macaulay's Miscellaneous Writings and Speeches.
Student's Edition. Crown 8vo. 6s.

Speeches of the Right Hon. Lord Macaulay, corrected by Himself.
People's Edition. Crown 8vo. 3s. 6d.

Lord Macaulay's Speeches on Parliamentary Reform in 1831 and 1832.
16mo. 1s.

The Rev. Sydney Smith's Essays contributed to the Edinburgh Review.
Authorised Edition, complete in One Volume, Crown 8vo. 2s. 6d. sewed, or 3s. 6d. cloth.

The Rev. Sydney Smith's Miscellaneous Works.
Crown 8vo. 6s.

The Wit and Wisdom of the Rev. Sydney Smith.
Crown 8vo. 3s. 6d.

The Miscellaneous Works of Thomas Arnold, D.D. Late Head Master of Rugby School and Regius Professor of Modern History in the Univ. of Oxford, collected and republished.
8vo. 7s. 6d.

Manual of English Literature, Historical and Critical. By Thomas Arnold, M.A.
New Edition. Crown 8vo. 7s. 6d.

Realities of Irish Life. By W. Steuart Trench.
Cr. 8vo. 2s. 6d. sewed, or 3s. 6d. cloth.

Lectures on the Science of Language. By F. Max Müller, M.A. &c.
Seventh Edition. 2 vols. crown 8vo. 16s.

Chips from a German Workshop; being Essays on the Science of Religion, and on Mythology, Traditions, and Customs. By F. Max Müller, M.A. &c.
3 vols. 8vo. £2.

Families of Speech.
Four Lectures delivered at
the Royal Institution.
By F. W. Farrar, M.A.
F.R.S.
New Edition. Crown 8vo. 3s. 6d.

Chapters on Language.
By F. W. Farrar, M.A.
F.R.S.
New Edition. Crown 8vo. 5s.

Southey's Doctor, com-
plete in One Volume.
Edited by Rev. J. W.
Warter, B.D.
Square crown 8vo. 12s. 6d.

A Budget of Paradoxes.
By Augustus De Morgan,
F.R.A.S.
Reprinted, with Author's Additions, from
the Athenæum. 8vo. 15s.

Recreations of a Country
Parson.
By A. K. H. B.
Two Series, 3s. 6d. each.

Landscapes, Churches,
and Moralities.
By A. K. H. B.
Crown 8vo. 3s. 6d.

Seaside Musings on Sun-
days and Weekdays.
By A. K. H. B.
Crown 8vo. 3s. 6d.

Changed Aspects of Un-
changed Truths.
By A. K. H. B.
Crown 8vo. 3s. 6d.

Counsel and Comfort
from a City Pulpit.
By A. K. H. B.
Crown 8vo. 3s. 6d.

Lessons of Middle Age.
By A. K. H. B.
Crown 8vo. 3s. 6d.

Leisure Hours in Town
By A. K. H. B.
Crown 8vo. 3s. 6d.

The Autumn Holidays
of a Country Parson.
By A. K. H. B.
Crown 8vo. 3s. 6d.

Sunday Afternoons at
the Parish Church of a
Scottish University City.
By A. K. H. B.
Crown 8vo. 3s. 6d.

The Commonplace Phi-
losopher in Town and
Country.
By A. K. H. B.
Crown 8vo. 3s. 6d.

Present-Day Thoughts.
By A. K. H. B.
Crown 8vo. 3s. 6d.

Critical Essays of a Country Parson.
By A. K. H. B.
Crown 8vo. 3s. 6d.

The Graver Thoughts of a Country Parson.
By A. K. H. B.
Two Series, 3s. 6d. each.

Principles of Education, drawn from Nature and Revelation, and applied to Female Education in the Upper Classes.
By the Author of 'Amy Herbert.'
2 vols. fcp. 8vo. 12s. 6d

From January to December; a Book for Children.
Second Edition. 8vo. 3s. 6d.

The Election of Representatives, Parliamentary and Municipal; a Treatise.
By Thos. Hare, Barrister.
Fourth Edition. Post 8vo. 7s.

Miscellaneous Writings of John Conington, M.A.
Edited by J. A. Symonds, M.A. With a Memoir by H. J. S. Smith, M.A.
2 vols. 8vo. 28s.

DICTIONARIES and OTHER BOOKS of REFERENCE.

A Dictionary of the English Language.
By R. G. Latham, M.A. M.D. F.R.S. Founded on the Dictionary of Dr. S. Johnson, as edited by the Rev. H. J. Todd, with numerous Emendations and Additions.
4 vols. 4to. £7.

Thesaurus of English Words and Phrases, classified and arranged so as to facilitate the expression of Ideas, and assist in Literary Composition.
By P. M. Roget, M.D.
Crown 8vo. 10s. 6d

English Synonymes.
By E. J. Whately. Edited by Archbishop Whately.
Fifth Edition. Fcp. 8vo. 3s.

A Practical Dictionary of the French and English Languages.
By Léon Contanseau, many years French Examiner for Military and Civil Appointments, &c.
Post 8vo. 10s. 6d.

Contanseau's Pocket Dictionary, French and English, abridged from the Practical Dictionary, by the Author.
Square 18mo. 3s. 6d.

New Practical Diction-
ary of the German Lan-
guage; German - English
and English-German.
  By Rev. W. L. Blackley,
  M.A. and Dr. C. M.
  Friedländer.
    Post 8vo. 7s. 6d.

A Dictionary of Roman
and Greek Antiquities.
With 2,000 Woodcuts
from Ancient Originals,
illustrative of the Arts
and Life of the Greeks and
Romans.
  By Anthony Rich, B.A.
    Third Edition. Crown 8vo. 7s. 6d.

The Mastery of Lan-
guages; or, the Art of
Speaking Foreign Tongues
Idiomatically.
  By Thomas Prendergast.
    Second Edition. 8vo. 6s.

A Practical English Dic-
tionary.
  By John T. White, D.D.
  Oxon. and T. C. Donkin,
  M.A.
1 vol. post 8vo. uniform with Contanseau's
Practical French Dictionary.
        [In the press.

A Latin-English Dic-
tionary.
  By John T. White, D.D.
  Oxon. and J. E. Riddle,
  M.A. Oxon.
    Third Edition, revised. 2 vols. 4to. 42s.

White's College Latin-
English Dictionary;
abridged from the Parent
Work for the use of Uni-
versity Students.
    Medium 8vo. 18s.

A Latin-English Dic-
tionary adapted for the use
of Middle-Class Schools,
  By John T. White, D.D.
  Oxon.
    Square fcp. 8vo. 3s.

White's Junior Student's
Complete Latin - English
and English-Latin Dic-
tionary.
    Square 12mo. 12s.

Separately { ENGLISH-LATIN, 5s. 6d.
           { LATIN-ENGLISH, 7s. 6d.

A Greek-English Lexi-
con.
  By H. G. Liddell, D.D.
  Dean of Christchurch,
  and R. Scott, D.D.
  Dean of Rochester.
    Sixth Edition. Crown 4to. 36s.

A Lexicon, Greek and
English, abridged for
Schools from Liddell and
Scott's Greek - English
Lexicon.
    Fourteenth Edition. Square 12mo. 7s. 6d.

An English-Greek Lexicon, containing all the Greek Words used by Writers of good authority.
By C. D. Yonge, B.A.
New Edition. 4to. 21s.

Mr. Yonge's New Lexicon, English and Greek, abridged from his larger Lexicon.
Square 12mo. 8s. 6d.

M'Culloch's Dictionary, Practical, Theoretical, and Historical, of Commerce and Commercial Navigation.
Edited by H. G. Reid.
8vo. 63s.

The Post Office Gazetteer of the United Kingdom: a Complete Dictionary of all Cities, Towns, Villages, and of the Principal Gentlemen's Seats, in Great Britain and Ireland, referred to the nearest Post Town, Railway & Telegraph Station; with Natural Features and Objects of Note.
By J. A. Sharp.
In 1 vol. 8vo. of about 1,500 pages.
[In the press.

A General Dictionary of Geography, Descriptive, Physical, Statistical, and Historical; forming a complete Gazetteer of the World.
By A. Keith Johnston, F.R.S.E.
New Edition, thoroughly revised.
[In the press.

The Public Schools Atlas of Modern Geography. In 31 Maps, exhibiting clearly the more important Physical Features of the Countries delineated.
Edited, with Introduction, by Rev. G. Butler, M.A.
Imperial quarto, 3s. 6d. sewed; 5s. cloth.

The Public Schools Manual of Modern Geography Forming a Companion to 'The Public Schools Atlas of Modern Geography.'
By Rev. G. Butler, M.A.
[In the press.

The Public Schools Atlas of Ancient Geography.
Edited, with an Introduction on the Study of Ancient Geography, by the Rev. G. Butler, M.A.
Imperial Quarto. [In the press.

ASTRONOMY and METEOROLOGY.

The Universe and the Coming Transits; Researches into and New Views respecting the Constitution of the Heavens.
By R. A. Proctor, B.A.
With 22 Charts and 22 Diagrams. 8vo. 16s.

The Transits of Venus; A Popular Account of Past and Coming Transits, from the first observed by Horrocks A.D. 1639 to the Transit of A.D. 2112.
By R. A. Proctor, B.A. Cantab.
With 20 Plates and numerous Woodcuts. Crown 8vo. [Nearly ready.

Essays on Astronomy. A Series of Papers on Planets and Meteors, the Sun and Sun-surrounding Space, Stars and Star Cloudlets.
By R. A. Proctor, B.A.
With 10 Plates and 24 Woodcuts. 8vo. 12s.

The Moon; her Motions, Aspect, Scenery, and Physical Condition.
By R. A. Proctor, B.A.
With Plates, Charts, Woodcuts, and Lunar Photographs. Crown 8vo. 15s.

The Sun; Ruler, Light, Fire, and Life of the Planetary System.
By R. A. Proctor, B.A.
Second Edition. Plates and Woodcuts. Cr. 8vo. 14s.

Saturn and its System.
By R. A. Proctor. B.A.
8vo. with 14 Plates, 14s.

The Orbs Around Us; a Series of Familiar Essays on the Moon and Planets, Meteors and Comets, the Sun and Coloured Pairs of Suns.
By R. A. Proctor, B.A.
Crown 8vo. 7s. 6d.

Other Worlds than Ours; The Plurality of Worlds Studied under the Light of Recent Scientific Researches.
By R. A. Proctor, B.A.
Third Edition, with 14 Illustrations. Cr. 8vo. 10s. 6d.

Brinkley's Astronomy. Revised and partly re-written, with Additional Chapters, and an Appendix of Questions for Examination.
By John W. Stubbs, D.D. Trin. Coll. Dublin and F. Brunnow, Ph.D. Astronomer Royal of Ireland.
With 49 Diagrams. Crown 8vo. 6s.

Outlines of Astronomy.
By Sir J. F. W. Herschel, Bart. M.A.
Latest Edition, with Plates and Diagrams. Square crown 8vo. 12s.

C

A New Star Atlas, for the Library, the School, and the Observatory, in 12 Circular Maps (with 2 Index Plates).
By R. A. Proctor, B.A.
Crown 8vo. 5s.

Celestial Objects for Common Telescopes.
By T. W. Webb, M.A. F.R.A.S.
New Edition, with Map of the Moon and Woodcuts. Crown 8vo. 7s. 6d.

Larger Star Atlas, for the Library, in Twelve Circular Maps, photolithographed by A. Brothers, F.R.A.S. With 2 Index Plates and a Letterpress Introduction.
By R. A. Proctor, BA.
Second Edition. Small folio, 25s.

Magnetism and Deviation of the Compass. For the use of Students in Navigation and Science Schools.
By J. Merrifield, LL.D.
18mo. 1s. 6d.

Dove's Law of Storms, considered in connexion with the ordinary Movements of the Atmosphere.
Translated by R. H. Scott, M.A.
8vo. 10s. 6d.

Air and Rain; the Beginnings of a Chemical Climatology.
By R. A. Smith, F.R.S.
8vo. 24s.

Nautical Surveying, an Introduction to the Practical and Theoretical Study of.
By J. K. Laughton, M.A.
Small 8vo. 6s.

Schellen's Spectrum Analysis, in its Application to Terrestrial Substances and the Physical Constitution of the Heavenly Bodies.
Translated by Jane and C. Lassell; edited, with Notes, by W. Huggins, LL.D. F.R.S.
With 13 Plates and 223 Woodcuts. 8vo. 28s.

NATURAL HISTORY and PHYSICAL SCIENCE.

The Correlation of Physical Forces.
By the Hon. Sir W. R. Grove, F.R.S. &c.
Sixth Edition, with other Contributions to Science. 8vo. 15s.

Professor Helmholtz' Popular Lectures on Scientific Subjects.
Translated by E. Atkinson, F.C.S.
With many Illustrative Wood Engravings. 8vo. 12s. 6d.

Ganot's Natural Philosophy for General Readers and Young Persons; a Course of Physics divested of Mathematical Formulæ and expressed in the language of daily life.

Translated by E. Atkinson, F.C.S.

Cr. 8vo. with 404 Woodcuts, 7s. 6d.

Ganot's Elementary Treatise on Physics, Experimental and Applied, for the use of Colleges and Schools.

Translated and edited by E. Atkinson, F.C.S.

New Edition, with a Coloured Plate and 726 Woodcuts. Post 8vo. 15s.

Principles of Animal Mechanics.

By the Rev. S. Haughton, F.R.S.

Second Edition. 8vo. 21s.

Weinhold's Introduction to Experimental Physics, Theoretical and Practical; including Directions for Constructing Physical Apparatus and for Making Experiments.

Translated by B. Loewy, F.R.A.S. With a Preface by G. C. Foster, F.R.S.

With numerous Woodcuts. 8vo.
[Nearly ready.

Text-Books of Science, Mechanical and Physical, adapted for the use of Artisans and of Students in Public and other Schools. (The first Ten edited by T. M. Goodeve, M.A. Lecturer on Applied Science at the Royal School of Mines; the remainder edited by C. W. Merrifield, F.R.S. an Examiner in the Department of Public Education.)

Small 8vo. Woodcuts.

Edited by T. M. Goodeve, M.A.

Anderson's *Strength of Materials*, 3s. 6d.
Bloxam's *Metals*, 3s. 6d.
Goodeve's *Mechanics*, 3s. 6d.
—— *Mechanism*, 3s. 6d.
Griffin's *Algebra & Trigonometry*, 3s. 6d.
  Notes on the same, with Solutions, 3s. 6d.
Jenkin's *Electricity & Magnetism*, 3s. 6d.
Maxwell's *Theory of Heat*, 3s. 6d.
Merrifield's *Technical Arithmetic*, 3s. 6d.
  Key, 3s. 6d.
Miller's *Inorganic Chemistry*, 3s. 6d.
Shelley's *Workshop Appliances*, 3s. 6d.
Watson's *Plane & Solid Geometry*, 3s. 6d.

Edited by C. W. Merrifield, F.R.S.

Armstrong's *Organic Chemistry*, 3s. 6d.
Thorpe's *Quantitative Analysis*, 4s. 6d.
Thorpe and Muir's *Qualitative Analysis*, 3s. 6d.

Address delivered before the British Association assembled at Belfast; with Additions and a Preface.

By John Tyndall, F.R.S. President.

8vo. price 3s.

Fragments of Science.

By John Tyndall, F.R.S.

Third Edition. 8vo. 14s.

Heat a Mode of Motion.
By *John Tyndall, F.R.S.*
Fourth Edition. Cr. 8vo. with Woodcuts, 10s. 6d.

Sound; a Course of Eight
Lectures delivered at the
Royal Institution of Great
Britain.
By *John Tyndall, F.R.S.*
Portrait and Woodcuts. Cr. 8vo. 9s.

Researches on Diamag-
netism and Magne-Crystal-
lic Action; including the
Question of Diamagnetic
Polarity.
By *John Tyndall, F.R.S.*
With 6 Plates and many Woodcuts, 8vo. 14s.

Contributions to Mole-
cular Physics in the do-
main of Radiant Heat.
By *John Tyndall, F.R.S.*
With 2 Plates and 31 Woodcuts. 8vo. 16s.

Lectures on Light, de-
livered in the United States
of America in 1872 and
1873.
By *J. Tyndall, F.R.S.*
Crown 8vo. 7s. 6d.

Notes of a Course of
Seven Lectures on Electri-
cal Phenomena and Theo-
ries, delivered at the Royal
Institution.
By *J. Tyndall, F.R.S.*
Crown 8vo. 1s. sewed, or 1s. 6d. cloth.

Notes of a Course of Nine
Lectures on Light, delivered
at the Royal Institution.
By *J. Tyndall, F.R.S.*
Crown 8vo. 1s. sewed, or 1s. 6d. cloth.

A Treatise on Magne-
tism, General and Terres-
trial.
By *Humphrey Lloyd,*
D.D. D.C.L. Provost of
Trinity College, Dublin.
8vo. price 10s. 6d.

Elementary Treatise on
the Wave-Theory of Light.
By *H. Lloyd, D.D. D.C.L.*
Third Edition. 8vo. 10s. 6d.

Professor Owen's Lec-
tures on the Comparative
Anatomy and Physiology
of Invertebrate Animals.
2nd Edition, with 235 Woodcuts. 8vo. 21s.

The Comparative Ana-
tomy and Physiology of the
Vertebrate Animals.
By *Richard Owen, F.R.S.*
With 1,472 Woodcuts. 3 vols. 8vo. £3. 13s. 6d.

Light Science for Lei-
sure Hours; a Series of
Familiar Essays on Scien-
tific Subjects, Natural Phenomena, &c.
By *R. A. Proctor, B.A.*
First and Second Series. 2 vols. crown 8vo.
7s. 6d. each.

*Kirby and Spence's In-
trodnction to Entomology,
or Elements of the Natural
History of Insects.*
Crown 8vo. 5s.

*Strange Dwellings; a De-
scription of the Habitations
of Animals, abridged from
'Homes without Hands.'
By Rev. J. G. Wood, M.A.*
With Frontispiece and 60 Woodcuts. Crown
8vo. 7s. 6d.

*Homes without Hands;
a Description of the Habitations of Animals, classed
according to their Principle
of Construction.
By Rev. J. G. Wood, M.A.*
With about 140 Vignettes on Wood. 8vo. 21s.

*Out of Doors; a Selec-
tion of Original Articles
on Practical Natural His-
tory.
By Rev. J. G. Wood, M.A.*
With 6 Illustrations from Original Designs
engraved on Wood. Crown 8vo. 7s. 6d.

*The Polar World: a
Popular Description of
Man and Nature in the
Arctic and Antarctic Re-
gions of the Globe.
By Dr. G. Hartwig.*
With Chromoxylographs, Maps, and Wood-
cuts. 8vo. 10s. 6d.

*The Sea and its Living
Wonders.
By Dr. G. Hartwig.*
Fourth Edition, enlarged. 8vo. with many
Illustrations, 10s. 6d.

*The Tropical World; a
Popular Scientific Account
of the Natural History of
the Equatorial Regions.
By Dr. G. Hartwig.*
With about 200 Illustrations. 8vo. 10s. 6d.

*The Subterranean World.
By Dr. G. Hartwig.*
With Maps and many Woodcuts. 8vo. 21s.

*The Aerial World.
By Dr. George Hartwig.*
With 8 Chromoxylographs and about 60
other Illustrations engraved on Wood.
8vo. price 21s.

*Insects at Home; a Popu-
lar Account of British
Insects, their Structure,
Habits, and Transforma-
tions.
By Rev. J. G. Wood, M.A.*
With upwards of 700 Woodcuts. 8vo. 21s.

*Insects Abroad; being a
Popular Account of Foreign
Insects, their Structure, Ha-
bits, and Transformations.
By Rev. J. G. Wood, M.A.*
With upwards of 700 Woodcuts. 8vo. 21s.

*A Familiar History of
Birds.
By E. Stanley, D.D. late
Ld. Bishop of Norwich.*
Fcp. 8vo. with Woodcuts, 3s. 6d.

Rocks Classified and Described.
By B. Von Cotta.
English Edition, by P. H. LAWRENCE (with English, German, and French Synonymes), revised by the Author. Post 8vo. 14s.

Primæval World of Switzerland.
By Professor Oswald Heer, of the University of Zurich. Translated by W. S. Dallas, F.L.S. and edited by James Heywood, M.A. F.R.S.
2 vols. 8vo. with numerous Illustrations. [In the press.

The Origin of Civilisation, and the Primitive Condition of Man; Mental and Social Condition of Savages.
By Sir J. Lubbock, Bart. M.P. F.R.S.
Third Edition, with 25 Woodcuts. 8vo. 16s.

A Manual of Anthropology, or Science of Man, based on Modern Research.
By Charles Bray.
Crown 8vo. 5s.

A Phrenologist amongst the Todas, or the Study of a Primitive Tribe in South India; History, Character, Customs, Religion, Infanticide, Polyandry, Language.
By W. E. Marshall, Lieut.-Col. Bengal Staff Corps.
With 26 Illustrations. 8vo. 21s.

The Ancient Stone Implements, Weapons, and Ornaments of Great Britain.
By John Evans, F.R.S.
With 2 Plates and 476 Woodcuts. 8vo. 28s.

The Elements of Botany for Families and Schools.
Tenth Edition, revised by Thomas Moore, F.L.S.
Fcp. 8vo. with 154 Woodcuts 2s. 6d.

Bible Animals; a Description of every Living Creature mentioned in the Scriptures, from the Ape to the Coral.
By Rev. J. G. Wood, M.A.
With about 100 Vignettes on Wood. 8vo. 21s.

The Rose Amateur's Guide.
By Thomas Rivers.
Tenth Edition. Fcp. 8vo. 4s.

A Dictionary of Science, Literature, and Art.
Fourth Edition, re-edited by the late W. T. Brande (the Author) and Rev. G. W. Cox, M.A.
3 vols. medium 8vo. 63s.

Loudon's Encyclopædia of Plants; comprising the Specific Character, Description, Culture, History, &c. of all the Plants found in Great Britain.
With upwards of 12,000 Woodcuts. 8vo. 42s.

The Treasury of Botany,
or Popular Dictionary of
the Vegetable Kingdom;
with which is incorporated
a Glossary of Botanical
Terms.
Edited by J. Lindley,
F.R.S. and T. Moore,
F.L.S.

With 274 Woodcuts and 20 Steel Plates.
Two Parts, fcp. 8vo. 12s.

**Handbook of Hardy
Trees, Shrubs, and Her-
baceous Plants;** containing
Descriptions &c. of the
Best Species in Cultivation;
with Cultural Details,
Comparative Hardiness,
suitability for particular
positions, &c. Based on
the French Work of De-
caisne and Naudin, and
including the 720 Original
Woodcut Illustrations.
By W. B. Hemsley.

Medium 8vo. 21s.

A General System of
Descriptive and Analytical
Botany.
Translated from the French
of Le Maout and De-
caisne, by Mrs. Hooker.
Edited and arranged
according to the English
Botanical System, by J.
D. Hooker, M.D. &c.
Director of the Royal
Botanic Gardens, Kew.

With 5,500 Woodcuts. Imperial 8vo. 52s. 6d.

**Forest Trees and Wood-
land Scenery,** as described
in Ancient and Modern
Poets.
By William Menzies, De-
puty Surveyor of Wind-
sor Forest and Parks, &c.

In One Volume, imperial 4to. with Twenty
Plates, Coloured in facsimile of the
original drawings, price £5. 5s.
[Preparing for publication.

CHEMISTRY and PHYSIOLOGY.

Miller's Elements of
Chemistry, Theoretical and
Practical.
Re-edited, with Additions,
by H. Macleod, F.C.S.
3 vols. 8vo. £3.
PART I. CHEMICAL PHYSICS, 15s.
PART II. INORGANIC CHEMISTRY, 21s.
PART III. ORGANIC CHEMISTRY, 24s.

**A Manual of Chemical
Physiology,** including its
Points of Contact with
Pathology.
By J. L. W. Thudichum,
M.D.

8vo. with Woodcuts, 7s. 6d.

A Dictionary of Chemistry and the Allied Branches of other Sciences. By Henry Watts, F.C.S. assisted by eminent Scientific and Practical Chemists.

6 vols. medium 8vo. £8. 14s. 6d.

Second Supplement completing the Record of Discovery to the end of 1872.

[In the press.

A Course of Practical Chemistry, for the use of Medical Students. By W. Odling, F.R.S.

Crown 8vo. Woodcuts, 7s. 6d.

Select Methods in Chemical Analysis, chiefly Inorganic. By Wm. Crookes, F.R.S.

With 22 Woodcuts. Crown 8vo. 12s. 6d.

Todd and Bowman's Physiological Anatomy, and Physiology of Man.

Vol. II. with numerous Illustrations, 25s.

Vol. I. New Edition by Dr. LIONEL S. BEALE, F.R.S. in course of publication, with numerous Illustrations. Parts I. and II. in 8vo. price 7s. 6d. each.

Outlines of Physiology, Human and Comparative. By J. Marshall, F.R.C.S. Surgeon to the University College Hospital.

2 vols. cr. 8vo. with 122 Woodcuts, 32s.

The FINE ARTS and ILLUSTRATED EDITIONS.

Albert Durer, his Life and Works; including Autobiographical Papers and Complete Catalogues. By William B. Scott.

With 6 Etchings by the Author and other Illustrations. 8vo. 16s.

In Fairyland; Pictures from the Elf-World. By Richard Doyle. With a Poem by W. Allingham.

With 16 coloured Plates, containing 36 Designs. Second Edition, folio, 15s.

A Dictionary of Artists of the English School: Painters, Sculptors, Architects, Engravers, and Ornamentists; with Notices of their Lives and Works. By Samuel Redgrave.

8vo. 16s.

The New Testament, illustrated with Wood Engravings after the Early Masters, chiefly of the Italian School.

Crown 4to. 63s.

The Life of Man Sym-
bolised by the Months of
the Year.
Text selected by R. Pigot.
25 Illustrations on Wood from Designs by
John Leighton, F.S.A. Quarto, 42s.

Lyra Germanica; the
Christian Year and the
Christian Life.
Translated by Miss C.
Winkworth.
With about 325 Woodcut Illustrations by J.
Leighton, F.S.A, and other Artists.
2 vols. 4to. price 42s.

Lord Macaulay's Lays
of Ancient Rome. With
90 Illustrations on Wood
from Drawings by G.
Scharf.
Fcp. 4to. 21s.

Miniature Edition, with
Scharf's 90 Illustrations
reduced in Lithography.
Imp. 16mo. 10s. 6d.

Sacred and Legendary
Art.
By Mrs. Jameson.
6 vols. square crown 8vo. price £5. 15s. 6d.
as follows:—

Legends of the Saints
and Martyrs.
New Edition, with 19 Etchings and 187
Woodcuts. 2 vols. 31s. 6d.

Legends of the Monastic
Orders.
New Edition, with 11 Etchings and 88
Woodcuts. 1 vol. 21s.

Legends of the Madonna.
New Edition, with 27 Etchings and 165
Woodcuts. 1 vol. 21s.

The History of Our Lord,
with that of his Types and
Precursors.
Completed by Lady East-
lake.
Revised Edition, with 13 Etchings and 281
Woodcuts. 2 vols. 42s.

The USEFUL ARTS, MANUFACTURES, &c.

A Manual of Architec-
ture: being a Concise History and Explanation of the
Principal Styles of Euro-
pean Architecture, Ancient,
Mediæval, and Renaissance;
with a Glossary.
By Thomas Mitchell, Au-
thor of 'The Stepping
Stone to Architecture.'
With 150 Woodcuts. Crown 8vo. 10s. 6d.

History of the Gothic
Revival; an Attempt to
shew how far the taste for
Mediæval Architecture was
retained in England during
the last two centuries, and
has been re-developed in the
present.
By Charles L. Eastlake,
Architect.
With 48 Illustrations. Imp. 8vo. 31s. 6d.

D

Industrial Chemistry; a Manual for Manufacturers and for Colleges or Technical Schools. Being a Translation of Professors Stohmann and Engler's German Edition of Payen's 'Précis de Chimie Industrielle,' by Dr. J. D. Barry. Edited, and supplemented with Chapters on the Chemistry of the Metals, by B. H. Paul, Ph.D.
8vo. with Plates and Woodcuts.
[In the press.

Gwilt's Encyclopædia of Architecture, with above 1,600 Woodcuts. Fifth Edition, with Alterations and Additions, by Wyatt Papworth.
8vo. 52s. 6d.

The Three Cathedrals dedicated to St. Paul in London; their History from the Foundation of the First Building in the Sixth Century to the Proposals for the Adornment of the Present Cathedral. By W. Longman, F.S.A.
With numerous Illustrations. Square crown 8vo. 21s.

Hints on Household Taste in Furniture, Upholstery, and other Details. By Charles L. Eastlake, Architect.
New Edition, with about 90 Illustrations. Square crown 8vo. 14s.

Geometric Turning; comprising a Description of Plant's New Geometric Chuck, with Directions for its use, and a Series of Patterns cut by it, with Explanations. By H. S. Savory.
With 571 Woodcuts. Square cr. 8vo. 21s.

Lathes and Turning, Simple, Mechanical, and Ornamental. By W. Henry Northcott.
With 240 Illustrations. 8vo. 18s.

Handbook of Practical Telegraphy. By R. S. Culley, Memb. Inst. C.E. Engineer-in-Chief of Telegraphs to the Post-Office.
Sixth Edition, Plates & Woodcuts. 8vo. 16s.

Principles of Mechanism, for the use of Students in the Universities, and for Engineering Students. By R. Willis, M.A. F.R.S. Professor in the University of Cambridge.
Second Edition, with 374 Woodcuts. 8vo. 18s.

Perspective; or, the Art of Drawing what one Sees: for the Use of those Sketching from Nature. By Lieut. W. H. Collins, R.E. F.R.A.S.
With 37 Woodcuts. Crown 8vo. 5s.

Encyclopædia of Civil Engineering, Historical, Theoretical, and Practical. By E. Cresy, C.E.
With about 3,000 Woodcuts. 8vo. 42s.

A Treatise on the Steam Engine, in its various applications to Mines, Mills, Steam Navigation, Railways and Agriculture. By J. Bourne, C.E.
With Portrait, 37 Plates, and 546 Woodcuts. 4to. 42s.

Catechism of the Steam Engine, in its various Applications. By John Bourne, C.E.
New Edition, with 89 Woodcuts. Fcp. 8vo. 6s.

Handbook of the Steam Engine. By J. Bourne, C.E. forming a KEY to the Author's Catechism of the Steam Engine.
With 67 Woodcuts. Fcp. 8vo. 9s.

Recent Improvements in the Steam Engine. By J. Bourne, C.E.
With 124 Woodcuts. Fcp. 8vo. 6s.

Lowndes's Engineer's Handbook; explaining the Principles which should guide the Young Engineer in the Construction of Machinery.
Post 8vo. 5s.

Ure's Dictionary of Arts, Manufactures, and Mines. Sixth Edition, re-written and greatly enlarged by R. Hunt, F.R.S. assisted by numerous Contributors.
With 2,000 Woodcuts. 3 vols. medium 8vo. £4. 14s. 6d.

Handbook to the Mineralogy of Cornwall and Devon; with Instructions for their Discrimination, and copious Tables of Locality. By J. H. Collins, F.G.S.
With 10 Plates. 8vo. 6s.

Guns and Steel; Miscellaneous Papers on Mechanical Subjects. By Sir J. Whitworth, C.E. F.R.S.
With Illustrations. Royal 8vo. 3s. 6d.

Practical Treatise on Metallurgy. Adapted from the last German Edition of Professor Kerl's Metallurgy by W. Crookes, F.R.S. &c. and E. Röhrig, Ph.D.
3 vols. 8vo. with 625 Woodcuts. £4. 19s.

Treatise on Mills and Millwork. By Sir W. Fairbairn, Bt.
With 18 Plates and 322 Woodcuts. 2 vols. 8vo. 32s.

Useful Information for Engineers.
By Sir W. Fairbairn, Bt.
With many Plates and Woodcuts. 3 vols. crown 8vo. 31s. 6d.

The Application of Cast and Wrought Iron to Building Purposes.
By Sir W. Fairbairn, Bt.
With 6 Plates and 118 Woodcuts. 8vo. 16s.

The Strains in Trusses Computed by means of Diagrams; with 20 Examples.
By F. A. Ranken, C.E.
With 35 Diagrams. Square cr. 8vo. 6s. 6d.

Practical Handbook of Dyeing and Calico-Printing.
By W. Crookes, F.R.S. &c.
With numerous Illustrations and Specimens of Dyed Textile Fabrics. 8vo. 42s.

Mitchell's Manual of Practical Assaying.
Fourth Edition, revised, with the Recent Discoveries incorporated, by W. Crookes, F.R.S.
8vo. Woodcuts, 31s. 6d.

Occasional Papers on Subjects connected with Civil Engineering, Gunnery, and Naval Architecture.
By Michael Scott, Memb. Inst. C.E. & of Inst. N.A.
2 vols. 8vo. with Plates, 42s.

London's Encyclopædia of Gardening : comprising the Theory and Practice of Horticulture, Floriculture, Arboriculture, and Landscape Gardening.
With 1,000 Woodcuts. 8vo. 21s.

London's Encyclopædia of Agriculture: comprising the Laying-out, Improvement, and Management of Landed Property, and the Cultivation and Economy of the Productions of Agriculture.
With 1,100 Woodcuts. 8vo. 21s.

RELIGIOUS and MORAL WORKS.

An Exposition of the 39 Articles, Historical and Doctrinal.
By E. H. Browne, D.D. Bishop of Winchester.
New Edition. 8vo. 16s.

An Introduction to the Theology of the Church of England, in an Exposition of the 39 Articles. By Rev. T. P. Boultbee, LL.D.
Fcp. 8vo. 6s.

Historical Lectures on the Life of Our Lord Jesus Christ.
By C. J. Ellicott, D.D.
Fifth Edition. 8vo. 12s.

Sermons; including Two Sermons on the Interpretation of Prophecy, and an Essay on the Right Interpretation and Understanding of the Scriptures.
By the late Rev. Thomas Arnold, D.D.
3 vols. 8vo. price 24s.

Christian Life, its Course, its Hindrances, and its Helps; Sermons preached mostly in the Chapel of Rugby School.
By the late Rev. Thomas Arnold, D.D.
8vo. 7s. 6d.

Christian Life, its Hopes, its Fears, and its Close; Sermons preached mostly in the Chapel of Rugby School.
By the late Rev. Thomas Arnold, D.D.
8vo. 7s. 6d.

Sermons Chiefly on the Interpretation of Scripture.
By the late Rev. Thomas Arnold, D.D.
8vo. price 7s. 6d.

Sermons preached in the Chapel of Rugby School; with an Address before Confirmation.
By the late Rev. Thomas Arnold, D.D.
Fcp. 8vo. price 3s. 6d.

Three Essays on Religion: Nature; the Utility of Religion; Theism.
By John Stuart Mill.
8vo. price 10s. 6d.

Synonyms of the Old Testament, their Bearing on Christian Faith and Practice.
By Rev. R. B. Girdlestone.
8vo. 15s.

Reasons of Faith; or, the Order of the Christian Argument Developed and Explained.
By Rev. G. S. Drew, M.A.
Second Edition. Fcp. 8vo. 6s.

The Eclipse of Faith: or a Visit to a Religious Sceptic.
By Henry Rogers.
Latest Edition. Fcp. 8vo. 5s.

Defence of the Eclipse of Faith.
By Henry Rogers.
Latest Edition. Fcp. 8vo. 3s. 6d.

Sermons for the Times preached in St. Paul's Cathedral and elsewhere.
By Rev. T. Griffith, M.A.
Crown 8vo. 6s.

The Life and Epistles of St. Paul.
By Rev. W. J. Conybeare, M.A. and Very Rev. J. S. Howson, D.D.
LIBRARY EDITION, with all the Original Illustrations, Maps, Landscapes on Steel, Woodcuts, &c. 2 vols. 4to. 48s.
INTERMEDIATE EDITION, with a Selection of Maps, Plates, and Woodcuts. 2 vols. square crown 8vo. 21s.
STUDENT'S EDITION, revised and condensed, with 46 Illustrations and Maps. 1 vol. crown 8vo. 9s.

A Critical and Grammatical Commentary on St. Paul's Epistles.
By C. J. Ellicott, D.D.
8vo. Galatians, 8s. 6d. Ephesians, 8s. 6d. Pastoral Epistles, 10s. 6d. Philippians, Colossians, & Philemon, 10s. 6d. Thessalonians, 7s. 6d.

The Voyage and Shipwreck of St. Paul; with Dissertations on the Ships and Navigation of the Ancients.
By James Smith, F.R.S.
Crown 8vo. Charts, 10s. 6d.

Evidence of the Truth of the Christian Religion derived from the Literal Fulfilment of Prophecy.
By Alexander Keith, D.D.
40th Edition, with numerous Plates. Square 8vo. 12s. 6d. or in post 8vo. with 5 Plates, 6s.

Historical and Critical Commentary on the Old Testament; with a New Translation.
By M. M. Kalisch, Ph.D.
Vol. I. Genesis, 8vo. 18s. or adapted for the General Reader, 12s. Vol. II. Exodus, 15s. or adapted for the General Reader, 12s. Vol. III. Leviticus, Part I. 15s. or adapted for the General Reader, 8s. Vol. IV. Leviticus, Part II. 15s. or adapted for the General Reader, 8s.

The History and Literature of the Israelites, according to the Old Testament and the Apocrypha.
By C. De Rothschild and A. De Rothschild.
Second Edition. 2 vols. crown 8vo. 12s. 6d. Abridged Edition, in 1 vol. fcp. 8vo. 3s. 6d.

Ewald's History of Israel.
Translated from the German by J. E. Carpenter, M.A. with Preface by R. Martineau, M.A.
5 vols. 8vo. 63s.

Commentary on Epistle to the Romans.
By Rev. W. A. O'Conor.
Crown 8vo. 3s. 6d.

A Commentary on the Gospel of St. John.
By Rev. W. A. O'Conor.
Crown 8vo. 10s. 6d.

The Epistle to the Hebrews; with Analytical Introduction and Notes.
By Rev. W. A. O'Conor.
Crown 8vo. 4s. 6d.

Thoughts for the Age.
By Elizabeth M. Sewell.
New Edition. Fcp. 8vo. 3s. 6d.

Passing Thoughts on Religion.
By Elizabeth M. Sewell.
Fcp. 8vo. 3s. 6d.

Self-examination before Confirmation.
By Elizabeth M. Sewell.
32mo. 1s. 6d.

Preparation for the Holy Communion; the Devotions chiefly from the works of Jeremy Taylor.
By Elizabeth M. Sewell.
32mo. 3s.

Readings for a Month Preparatory to Confirmation, from Writers of the Early and English Church.
By Elizabeth M. Sewell.
Fcp. 8vo. 4s.

Readings for Every Day in Lent, compiled from the Writings of Bishop Jeremy Taylor.
By Elizabeth M. Sewell.
Fcp. 8vo. 5s.

Bishop Jeremy Taylor's Entire Works; with Life by Bishop Heber.
Revised and corrected by the Rev. C. P. Eden.
10 vols. £5. 5s.

Hymns of Praise and Prayer.
Collected and edited by Rev. J. Martineau, LL.D.
Crown 8vo. 4s. 6d.

Thoughts for the Holy Week, for Young Persons.
By Elizabeth M. Sewell.
New Edition. Fcp. 8vo. 2s.

Spiritual Songs for the Sundays and Holidays throughout the Year.
By J. S. B. Monsell, LL.D.
Fourth Edition. Fcp. 8vo. 4s. 6d.

Lyra Germanica; Hymns translated from the German by Miss C. Winkworth.
2 series, fcp. 8vo. 3s. 6d. each.

Endeavours after the Christian Life; Discourses.
By Rev. J. Martineau, LL.D.
Fifth Edition. Crown 8vo. 7s. 6d.

An Introduction to the Study of the New Testament, Critical, Exegetical, and Theological.
By Rev. S. Davidson, D.D.
2 vols. 8vo. 30s.

Supernatural Religion; an Inquiry into the Reality of Divine Revelation.
New Edition. 2 vols. 8vo. 24s.

The Life of Christ.
For the use of Young Persons, selected from the Gospels and Chronologically arranged; with Supplementary Notices from parallel Passages.
By the Rev. R. B. Gardiner, M.A.
Crown 8vo. 2s.

Lectures on the Pentateuch & the Moabite Stone;
with Appendices.
By J. W. Colenso, D.D.
Bishop of Natal.
8vo. 12s.

The Pentateuch and Book of Joshua Critically Examined.
By J. W. Colenso, D.D.
Bishop of Natal.
Crown 8vo. 6s.

**The New Bible Commentary, by Bishops and other Clergy of the Anglican Church, critically examined by the Rt. Rev. J. W. Colenso, D.D.
Bishop of Natal.**
8vo. 25s.

TRAVELS, VOYAGES, &c.

The Valleys of Tirol;
their Traditions and Customs, and How to Visit them.
By Miss R. H. Busk, Author of 'The Folk-Lore of Rome' &c.
With Frontispiece and 3 Maps. Crown 8vo. 12s. 6d.

Eight Years in Ceylon.
By Sir Samuel W. Baker, M.A. F.R.G.S.
New Edition, with Illustrations engraved on Wood by G. Pearson. Crown 8vo. Price 7s. 6d.

The Rifle and the Hound in Ceylon.
By Sir Samuel W. Baker, M.A. F.R.G.S.
New Edition, with Illustrations engraved on Wood by G. Pearson. Crown 8vo. Price 7s. 6d.

Meeting the Sun; a Journey all round the World through Egypt, China, Japan, and California.
By William Simpson, F.R.G.S.
With Heliotypes and Woodcuts. 8vo. 24s.

The Rural Life of England.
By William Howitt.
Woodcuts, 8vo. 12s. 6d.

The Dolomite Mountains. Excursions through Tyrol, Carinthia, Carniola, and Friuli.
By J. Gilbert and G. C. Churchill, F.R.G.S.
With Illustrations. Sq. cr. 8vo. 21s.

The *Alpine Club Map of the Chain of Mont Blanc, from an actual Survey in 1863-1864.*
By A. Adams-Reilly, F.R.G.S. M.A.C.

In Chromolithography, on extra stout drawing paper 10s. or mounted on canvas in a folding case, 12s. 6d.

The *Alpine Club Map of the Valpelline, the Val Tournanche, and the Southern Valleys of the Chain of Monte Rosa, from actual Survey.*
By A. Adams-Reilly, F.R.G.S. M.A.C.

Price 6s. on extra Stout Drawing Paper, or 7s. 6d. mounted in a Folding Case.

Hours of Exercise in the Alps.
By John Tyndall, F.R.S.

Third Edition, with 7 Woodcuts by E. Whymper. Crown 8vo. 12s. 6d.

Guide to the Pyrenees, for the use of Mountaineers.
By Charles Packe.

Second Edition, with Maps &c. and Appendix. Crown 8vo. 7s. 6d.

How to See Norway.
By J. R. Campbell.

With Map and 5 Woodcuts, fcp. 8vo. 5s.

Untrodden Peaks and Unfrequented Valleys; a Midsummer Ramble among the Dolomites.
By Amelia B. Edwards.

With numerous Illustrations. 8vo. 21s.

The *Alpine Club Map of Switzerland, with parts of the Neighbouring Countries, on the scale of four miles to an Inch.*
Edited by R. C. Nichols, F.S.A. F.R.G.S.

In Four Sheets, in Portfolio, 42s. or mounted in a Case, 52s. 6d. Each Sheet may be had separately, price 12s. or mounted in a Case, 15s.

The Alpine Guide.
By John Ball, M.R.I.A. late President of the Alpine Club.

Post 8vo. with Maps and other Illustrations.

Eastern Alps.
Price 10s. 6d.

Central Alps, including all the Oberland District.
Price 7s. 6d.

Western Alps, including Mont Blanc, Monte Rosa, Zermatt, &c.
Price 6s. 6d.

Introduction on Alpine Travelling in general, and on the Geology of the Alps.
Price 1s. Either of the Three Volumes or Parts of the 'Alpine Guide' may be had with this Introduction prefixed, 1s. extra.

Visits to Remarkable Places, and Scenes illustrative of striking Passages in English History and Poetry.
By William Howitt.

2 vols. 8vo. Woodcuts, 25s.

E

WORKS of FICTION.

*Whispers from Fairy-
land.*
   By the Rt. Hon. E. H.
   Knatchbull - Hugessen,
   M.P. Author of 'Stories
   for my Children,' 'Moon-
   shine,' 'Queer Folk,' &c.
   *With 9 Illustrations from Original De-
   signs engraved on Wood by G. Pearson. Crown 8vo. price 6s.*

Elena, an Italian Tale.
   By L. N. Comyn.
   2 vols. post 8vo. 14s.

*Lady   Willoughby's
   Diary during the Reign of
   Charles the First, the Pro-
   tectorate, and the Restora-
   tion.*
   Crown 8vo. 7s. 6d.

Centulle, a Tale of Pau.
   By Denys Shyne Lawlor,
   Author of 'Pilgrimages in
   the Pyrenees and Landes.'
   Crown 8vo. 10s. 6d.

*The Folk-Lore of Rome,
   collected by Word of Mouth
   from the People.*
   By R. H. Busk, Author of
   'The Valleys of Tirol'
   &c.
   Crown 8vo. 12s. 6d.

*Cyllene; or, The Fall of
   Paganism.*
   By Henry Sneyd, M.A.
   2 vols. post 8vo. 14s.

*Tales of the Teutonic
   Lands.*
   By Rev. G. W. Cox, M.A.
   and E. H. Jones.
   Crown 8vo. 10s. 6d.

*Becker's Gallus; or Ro-
   man Scenes of the Time of
   Augustus.*
   Post 8vo. 7s. 6d.

*Becker's Charicles: Il-
   lustrative of Private Life
   of the Ancient Greeks.*
   Post 8vo. 7s. 6d.

Tales of Ancient Greece.
   By the Rev. G. W. Cox,
   M.A.
   Crown 8vo. 6s. 6d.

*The Modern Novelist's
   Library.*

Atherstone Priory, 2s. boards; 2s. 6d. cloth.
*The Burgomaster's Family, 2s. boards;
   2s. 6d. cloth.*
MELVILLE'S *Digby Grand, 2s. and 2s. 6d.*
———— *Gladiators, 2s. and 2s.6d.*
———— *Good for Nothing, 2s. & 2s. 6d.*
———— *Holmby House, 2s. and 2s. 6d.*
———— *Interpreter, 2s. and 2s. 6d.*
———— *Kate Coventry, 2s. and 2s. 6d.*
———— *Queen's Maries, 2s. and 2s. 6d.*
———— *General Bounce, 2s. and 2s. 6d.*
TROLLOPE'S *Warden, 1s. 6d. and 2s.*
———— *Barchester Towers, 2s. and
   2s. 6d.*
BRAMLEY-MOORE'S *Six Sisters of the Val-
   leys, 2s. boards; 2s. 6d. cloth.*

Novels and Tales.
By the Right Hon. Benjamin Disraeli, M.P.

Cabinet Editions, complete in Ten Volumes, crown 8vo. 6s. each, as follows:—

Lothair, 6s.
Coningsby, 6s.
Sybil, 6s.
Tancred, 6s.
Henrietta Temple, 6s.
Contarini Fleming, &c. 6s.

Venetia, 6s.
Alroy, Ixion, &c. 6s.
Young Duke, &c. 6s.
Vivian Grey, 6s.

Cabinet Edition, in crown 8vo. of Stories and Tales by Miss Sewell :—

Amy Herbert, 2s. 6d.
Gertrude, 2s. 6d.
Earl's Daughter, 2s. 6d.
Experience of Life, 2s. 6d.
Cleve Hall, 2s. 6d.

Ivors, 2s. 6d.
Katharine Ashton, 2s. 6d.
Margaret Percival, 3s. 6d.
Laneton Parsonage, 3s. 6d.
Ursula, 3s. 6d.

POETRY and THE DRAMA.

Ballads and Lyrics of Old France; with other Poems.
By A. Lang.
Square fcp. 8vo. 5s.

Moore's Lalla Rookh,
Tenniel's Edition, with 68 Wood Engravings.
Fcp. 4to. 21s.

Moore's Irish Melodies,
Maclise's Edition, with 161 Steel Plates.
Super-royal 8vo. 31s. 6d.

Miniature Edition of Moore's Irish Melodies, with Maclise's 161 Illustrations reduced in Lithography.
Imp. 16mo. 10s. 6d.

Milton's Lycidas and Epitaphium Damonis.
Edited, with Notes and Introduction, by C. S. Jerram, M.A.
Crown 8vo. 3s. 6d.

Lays of Ancient Rome; with Ivry and the Armada.
By the Right Hon. Lord Macaulay.
16mo. 3s. 6d.

Lord Macaulay's Lays of Ancient Rome. With 90 Illustrations on Wood from Drawings by G. Scharf.
Fcp. 4to. 21s.

Miniature Edition of Lord Macaulay's Lays of Ancient Rome, with Scharf's 90 Illustrations reduced in Lithography.
Imp. 16mo. 10s. 6d.

Southey's Poetical Works with the Author's last Corrections and Additions.
Medium 8vo. with Portrait, 14s.

Bowdler's Family Shakspeare, cheaper Genuine Edition.
Complete in 1 vol. medium 8vo. large type, with 36 Woodcut Illustrations, 14s. or in 6 vols. fcp. 8vo. price 21s.

Horatii Opera, Library
Edition, with English
Notes, Marginal References
and various Readings.
Edited by Rev. J. E. Yonge.
8vo. 21s.

The Æneid of Virgil
Translated into English
Verse.
By J. Conington, M.A.
Crown 8vo. 9s.

Poems by Jean Ingelow.
2 vols. Fcp. 8vo. 10s.

FIRST SERIES, containing 'Divided,' 'The
Star's Monument,' &c. 16th Thousand.
Fcp. 8vo. 5s.

SECOND SERIES, 'A Story of Doom,' 'Gla-
dys and her Island,' &c. 5th Thousand.
Fcp. 8vo. 5s.

Poems by Jean Ingelow.
First Series, with nearly
100 Woodcut Illustrations.
Fcp. 4to. 21s.

RURAL SPORTS, HORSE and CATTLE MANAGEMENT, &c.

Down the Road; or,
Reminiscences of a Gentle-
man Coachman.
By C. T. S. Birch Rey-
nardson.
With Twelve Chromolithographic Illustra-
tions from Original Paintings by H.
Alken. Medium 8vo. [Nearly ready.

Blaine's Encyclopædia of
Rural Sports; Complete
Accounts, Historical, Prac-
tical, and Descriptive, of
Hunting, Shooting, Fish-
ing, Racing, &c.
With above 600 Woodcuts (20 from Designs
by JOHN LEECH). 8vo. 21s.

A Book on Angling:
a Treatise on the Art of
Angling in every branch,
including full Illustrated
Lists of Salmon Flies.
By Francis Francis.
Post 8vo. Portrait and Plates, 15s.

Wilcocks's Sea-Fisher-
man: comprising the Chief
Methods of Hook and Line
Fishing, a glance at Nets,
and remarks on Boats and
Boating.
New Edition, with 80 Woodcuts.
Post 8vo. 12s. 6d.

The Ox, his Diseases and
their Treatment; with an
Essay on Parturition in the
Cow.
By J. R. Dobson, Memb.
R.C.V.S.
Crown 8vo. with Illustrations, 7s. 6d.

A Treatise on Horse-
Shoeing and Lameness.
By J. Gamgee, Vet. Surg.
8vo. with 55 Woodcuts, 10s. 6d.

Youatt on the Horse.
Revised and enlarged by W.
Watson, M.R.C.V.S.
8vo. Woodcuts, 12s. 6d.

Youatt's Work on the Dog, revised and enlarged.
8vo. Woodcuts, 6s.

Horses and Stables.
By Colonel F. Fitzwygram, XV. the King's Hussars.
With 24 Plates of Illustrations. 8vo. 10s. 6d.

The Dog in Health and Disease.
By Stonehenge.
With 73 Wood Engravings. Square crown 8vo. 7s. 6d.

The Greyhound.
By Stonehenge.
Revised Edition, with 24 Portraits of Greyhounds. Square crown 8vo. 10s. 6d.

Stables and Stable Fittings.
By W. Miles, Esq.
Imp. 8vo. with 13 Plates, 15s.

The Horse's Foot, and how to keep it Sound.
By W. Miles, Esq.
Ninth Edition. Imp. 8vo. Woodcuts, 12s. 6d.

A Plain Treatise on Horse-shoeing.
By W. Miles, Esq.
Sixth Edition. Post 8vo. Woodcuts, 2s. 6d.

Remarks on Horses' Teeth, addressed to Purchasers.
By W. Miles, Esq.
Post 8vo. 1s. 6d.

The Fly-Fisher's Entomology.
By Alfred Ronalds.
With coloured Representations of the Natural and Artificial Insect.
With 20 coloured Plates. 8vo. 14s.

The Dead Shot, or Sportsman's Complete Guide; a Treatise on the Use of the Gun, Dog-breaking, Pigeon-shooting, &c.
By Marksman.
Fcp. 8vo. with Plates, 5s.

WORKS of UTILITY and GENERAL INFORMATION.

Maunder's Treasury of Knowledge and Library of Reference; comprising an English Dictionary and Grammar, Universal Gazetteer, Classical Dictionary, Chronology, Law Dictionary, Synopsis of the Peerage, Useful Tables, &c.

Fcp. 8vo. 6s.

Maunder's Biographical Treasury.
Latest Edition, reconstructed and partly rewritten, with about 1,000 additional Memoirs, by W. L. R. Cates.

Fcp. 8vo. 6s.

Maunder's Scientific and Literary Treasury; a Popular Encyclopædia of Science, Literature, and Art.
New Edition, in part rewritten, with above 1,000 new articles, by J. Y. Johnson.

Fcp. 8vo. 6s.

Maunder's Treasury of Geography, Physical, Historical, Descriptive, and Political.
Edited by W. Hughes, F.R.G.S.

With 7 Maps and 16 Plates. Fcp. 8vo. 6s.

Maunder's Historical Treasury; General Introductory Outlines of Universal History, and a Series of Separate Histories.
Revised by the Rev. G. W. Cox, M.A.

Fcp. 8vo. 6s.

Maunder's Treasury of Natural History; or Popular Dictionary of Zoology.

Revised and corrected Edition. Fcp. 8vo. with 900 Woodcuts, 6s.

The Treasury of Bible Knowledge; being a Dictionary of the Books, Persons, Places, Events, and other Matters of which mention is made in Holy Scripture.
By Rev. J. Ayre, M.A.

With Maps, 15 Plates, and numerous Woodcuts. Fcp. 8vo. 6s.

Collieries and Colliers: a Handbook of the Law and Leading Cases relating thereto.
By J. C. Fowler.

Third Edition. Fcp. 8vo. 7s. 6d.

The Theory and Practice of Banking.
By H. D. Macleod, M.A.

Second Edition. 2 vols. 8vo. 30s.

Modern Cookery for Private Families, reduced to a System of Easy Practice in a Series of carefully-tested Receipts.
By Eliza Acton.
With 8 Plates & 150 Woodcuts. Fcp. 8vo. 6s.

A Practical Treatise on Brewing; with Formulæ for Public Brewers, and Instructions for Private Families.
By W. Black.
Fifth Edition. 8vo. 10s. 6d.

Three Hundred Original Chess Problems and Studies.
By Jas. Pierce, M.A. and W. T. Pierce.
With many Diagrams. Sq. fcp. 8vo. 7s. 6d. Supplement, 2s. 6d.

Chess Openings.
By F. W. Longman, Balliol College, Oxford.
Second Edition, revised. Fcp. 8vo. 2s. 6d.

The Theory of the Modern Scientific Game of Whist.
By W. Pole, F.R.S.
Fifth Edition. Fcp. 8vo. 2s. 6d.

The Cabinet Lawyer; a Popular Digest of the Laws of England, Civil, Criminal, and Constitutional.
Twenty-fourth Edition, corrected and extended. Fcp. 8vo. 9s.

Blackstone Economised; being a Compendium of the Laws of England to the Present Time.
By D. M. Aird, Barrister.
Revised Edition. Post 8vo. 7s. 6d.

Pewtner's Comprehensive Specifier; a Guide to the Practical Specification of every kind of Building-Artificer's Work.
Edited by W. Young.
Crown 8vo. 6s.

Hints to Mothers on the Management of their Health during the Period of Pregnancy and in the Lying-in Room.
By Thomas Bull, M.D.
Fcp. 8vo. 5s.

The Maternal Management of Children in Health and Disease.
By Thomas Bull, M.D.
Fcp. 8vo. 5s.

KNOWLEDGE for the YOUNG.

The Stepping-Stone to Knowledge; or upwards of 700 Questions and Answers on Miscellaneous Subjects, adapted to the capacity of Infant minds.
18mo. 1s.

Second Series of the Stepping-Stone to Knowledge: Containing upwards of 800 Questions and Answers on Miscellaneous Subjects not contained in the First Series.
18mo. 1s.

The Stepping-Stone to Geography: Containing several Hundred Questions and Answers on Geographical Subjects.
18mo. 1s.

The Stepping-Stone to English History; Questions and Answers on the History of England.
18mo. 1s.

The Stepping-Stone to Bible Knowledge; Questions and Answers on the Old and New Testaments.
18mo. 1s.

The Stepping-Stone to Biography; Questions and Answers on the Lives of Eminent Men and Women.
18mo. 1s.

The Stepping-Stone to Irish History: Containing several Hundred Questions and Answers on the History of Ireland.
18mo. 1s.

The Stepping-Stone to French History: Containing several Hundred Questions and Answers on the History of France.
18mo. 1s.

The Stepping-Stone to Roman History: Containing several Hundred Questions and Answers on the History of Rome.
18mo. 1s.

The Stepping-Stone to Grecian History: Containing several Hundred Questions and Answers on the History of Greece.
18mo. 1s.

The Stepping-Stone to English Grammar: Containing several Hundred Questions and Answers on English Grammar.
18mo. 1s.

The Stepping-Stone to French Pronunciation and Conversation: Containing several Hundred Questions and Answers.
18mo. 1s.

The Stepping-Stone to Astronomy: Containing several Hundred familiar Questions and Answers on the Earth and the Solar and Stellar Systems.
18mo. 1s.

The Stepping-Stone to Music: Containing several Hundred Questions on the Science; also a short History of Music.
18mo. 1s.

The Stepping-Stone to Natural History: Vertebrate or Backboned Animals. Part I. Mammalia; Part II. Birds, Reptiles, Fishes.
18mo. 1s. each Part.

The Stepping-Stone to Architecture; Questions and Answers explaining the Principles and Progress of Architecture from the Earliest Times.
With 100 Woodcuts. 18mo. 1s.

INDEX.

Acton's Modern Cookery 39
Aird's Blackstone Economised 39
Alpine Club Map of Switzerland 33
Alpine Guide (The) 33
Amos's Jurisprudence 10
——— Primer of the Constitution 10
Anderson's Strength of Materials 20
Armstrong's Organic Chemistry 20
Arnold's (Dr.) Christian Life 29
——— Lectures on Modern History ... 2
——— Miscellaneous Works 12
——— School Sermons 29
——— Sermons 29
——— (T.) Manual of English Literature 12
Arnould's Life of Lord Denman 7
Atherstone Priory 39
Autumn Holidays of a Country Parson ... 13
Ayre's Treasury of Bible Knowledge 28

Bacon's Essays, by *Whately* 10
——— Life and Letters, by *Spedding* ... 10
——— Works 10
Bain's Mental and Moral Science 11
——— on the Senses and Intellect 11
Baker's Two Works on Ceylon 32
Ball's Guide to the Central Alps 38
——— Guide to the Western Alps 38
——— Guide to the Eastern Alps 38
Becker's Charicles and Gallus 34
Black's Treatise on Brewing 39
Blackley's German-English Dictionary 15
Blaine's Rural Sports 36
Blossom's Metals 20
Boultbee on 39 Articles 28
Bourne's Catechism of the Steam Engine . 27
——— Handbook of Steam Engine...... 27
——— Treatise on the Steam Engine ... 27
——— Improvements in the same...... 27
Bowdler's Family *Shakspeare* 35
Bramley-Moore's Six Sisters of the Valley . 39
Brande's Dictionary of Science, Literature,
   and Art 22
Bray's Manual of Anthropology 22
——— Philosophy of Necessity 11
Brinkley's Astronomy 17
Browne's Exposition of the 39 Articles...... 28
Brunel's Life of *Brunel* 7
Buckle's History of Civilisation 3
——— Posthumous Remains 12
Bull's Hints to Mothers 39
——— Maternal Management of Children.. 39
Burgomaster's Family (The) 39

Burke's Rise of Great Families 8
——— Vicissitudes of Families............. 8
Bull's Folk-lore of Rome 34
——— Valleys of Tirol 32

Cabinet Lawyer...................................... 39
Campbell's Norway 33
Cates's Biographical Dictionary.............. 8
——— and *Woodward's* Encyclopædia ... 5
Changed Aspects of Unchanged Truths 13
Chesney's Indian Polity 3
——— Modern Military Biography..... 3
——— Waterloo Campaign 3
Clough's Lives from Plutarch................. 4
Colenso on Moabite Stone &c. 12
——— 's Pentateuch and Book of Joshua. 12
——— Speaker's Bible Commentary ... 12
Collins's Mineralogy of Cornwall 27
——— Perspective.............................. 26
Commonplace Philosopher in Town and
   Country, by A. K. H. B. 13
Comte's Positive Polity 7
Comyn's Elena 34
Congreve's Essays 9
——— Politics of Aristotle 10
Conington's Translation of Virgil's Æneid 26
——— Miscellaneous Writings.......... 14
Contanseau's Two French Dictionaries ... 14
Conybeare and *Howson's* Life and Epistles
   of St. Paul 29
Cotton's Memoir and Correspondence 7
Counsel and Comfort from a City Pulpit.... 13
Cox's (G. W.) Aryan Mythology 4
——— Crusades 6
——— History of Greece 4
——— Tale of the Great Persian
   War... 4
——— Tales of Ancient Greece 34
——— and *Jones's* Teutonic Tales 34
Crawley's Thucydides 4
Cresy on British Constitution 3
Cresy's Encyclopædia of Civil Engineering 27
Critical Essays of a Country Parson.......... 14
Crookes's Chemical Analysis 24
——— Dyeing and Calico-printing......... 28
Culley's Handbook of Telegraphy............. 26
Cusack's Student's History of Ireland 3

D'Aubigné's Reformation in the Time of
   Calvin 6

Davidson's Introduction to New Testament 31
Dead Shot (The), by Marksman 37
De Caisne and Le Maout's Botany 23
De Morgan's Paradoxes 13
De Tocqueville's Democracy in America... 9
Disraeli's Lord George Bentinck 7
———— Novels and Tales 35
Dobson on the Ox 36
Dove's Law of Storms 18
Doyle's Fairyland 24
Drew's Reasons of Faith.................... 29

Rawlske's Gothic Revival 25
———— Hints on Household Taste...... 66
Edwards's Rambles among the Dolomites 33
Elements of Botany........................ 23
Ellicott's Commentary on Ephesians 30
————————— Galatians 30
————————— Pastoral Epist. 30
————————— Philippians &c. 30
————————— Thessalonians . 30
———— Lectures on Life of Christ 29
Epochs of History 6
Evans's Ancient Stone Implements 22
Ewald's History of Israel 30

Fairbairn's Application of Cast and
            Wrought Iron to Building... 28
———— Information for Engineers.... 28
———— Treatise on Mills and Millwork 27
Farrar's Chapters on Language 13
———— Families of Speech 13
Fitzwygram on Horses and Stables......... 37
Forsyth's Essays 9
Fowler's Collieries and Colliers 38
Francis's Fishing Book 36
Freeman's Historical Geography of Europe 5
From January to December 14
Froude's English in Ireland 2
———— History of England 2
———— Short Studies................. 12

Gairdner's Houses of Lancaster and York 6
Gamgee on Horse-Shoeing 96
Ganot's Elementary Physics 19
———— Natural Philosophy 19
Gardiner's Buckingham and Charles 3
———— Life of Christ 32
———— Thirty Years' War 6
Gilbert and Churchill's Dolomites 32
Girdlestone's Bible Synonyms.............. 29
Goodeve's Mechanics 20
———— Mechanism 20
Grant's Ethics of Aristotle 10
Graver Thoughts of a Country Parson..... 14
Greville's Journal 2
Griffin's Algebra and Trigonometry....... 20
Griffith's Sermons for the Times 29
Grove on Correlation of Physical Forces.. 18
Gwilt's Encyclopædia of Architecture..... 26

Hare on Election of Representatives 14

Harrison's Political Problems 8
Hartwig's Aerial World 21
———— Polar World 21
———— Sea and Its Living Wonders .. 21
———— Subterranean World.......... 21
———— Tropical World 21
Haughton's Animal Mechanics 19
Hayward's Biographical and Critical Essays 7
Herr's Switzerland 22
Helmholtz's Scientific Lectures 18
Helmsley's Trees, Shrubs, and Herbaceous
         Plants 23
Herschel's Outlines of Astronomy 17
Holland's Recollections 7
Howitt's Rural Life of England 32
———— Visits to Remarkable Places .. 33
Humboldt's Life........................... 7
Hume's Essays 11
———— Treatise on Human Nature...... 11

Ihne's History of Rome 5
Ingelow's Poems 36

Jameson's Legends of Saints and Martyrs . 25
———— Legends of the Madonna...... 25
———— Legends of the Monastic Orders 25
———— Legends of the Saviour........ 25
Jenkin's Electricity and Magnetism........ 20
Jerram's Lycidas of Milton 35
Jerrold's Life of Napoleon 1
Johnston's Geographical Dictionary........ 17

Kalisch's Commentary on the Bible 30
Keith's Evidence of Prophecy 30
Kenyon's (Lord) Life...................... 7
Kerl's Metallurgy, by Crookes and Röhrig. 37
Kirby and Spence's Entomology 21
Knatchbull-Hugessen's Whispers from
         Fairy-Land 24

Landscapes, Churches, &c. by A. K. H. B. 13
Lang's Ballads and Lyrics 35
Latham's English Dictionary.............. 14
Laughton's Nautical Surveying 18
Lawlor's Centulle.......................... 34
Lawrence on Rocks 22
Lecky's History of European Morals....... 5
———— Rationalism 5
———— Leaders of Public Opinion.... 7
Leisure Hours in Town, by A. K. H. B.. 13
Lessons of Middle Age, by A. K. H. B.... 13
Lewes's Biographical History of Philosophy 5
Liddell and Scott's Greek-English Lexicons 15
Life of Man Symbolised 25
Lindley and Moore's Treasury of Botany... 23
Lloyd's Magnetism 20
———— Wave-Theory of Light 20

Longman's Chess Openings.................. 39
———— Edward the Third 3
———— Lectures on History of England 3
———— Old and New St. Paul's.......... 26
London's Encyclopædia of Agriculture ... 28
———————— Gardening...... 28
———————— Plants......... 22
Lowndes's Engineer's Handbook 27
Lubbock's Origin of Civilisation 22
Lyra Germanica 25, 31

Macaulay's (Lord) Essays 2
———————— History of England ... 2
———————— Lays of Ancient Rome 25, 35
———————— Miscellaneous Writings 12
———————— Speeches 12
———————— Works 2
McCulloch's Dictionary of Commerce 16
Macleod's Principles of Economical Philosophy 10
———————— Theory and Practice of Banking 38
Markham's History of Persia................. 4
Marshall's Physiology..................... 24
———————— Todas..................... 22
Marshman's History of India.............. 3
———————— Life of Havelock 8
Martineau's Christian Life................ 31
———————— Hymns................. 31
Maunder's Biographical Treasury........... 38
———————— Geographical Treasury 38
———————— Historical Treasury 38
———————— Scientific and Literary Treasury 38
———————— Treasury of Knowledge 38
———————— Treasury of Natural History ... 38
Maxwell's Theory of Heat................. 20
May's History of Democracy............... 2
———————— History of England 2
Melville's Digby Grand 39
———————— General Bounce 39
———————— Gladiators 39
———————— Good for Nothing 39
———————— Holmby House 39
———————— Interpreter 39
———————— Kate Coventry 39
———————— Queen's Maries 39
Mendelssohn's Letters 8
Menteith's Forest Trees and Woodland Scenery 23
Merivale's Fall of the Roman Republic ... 4
———————— Romans under the Empire 4
Merrifield's Arithmetic and Mensuration... 20
———————— Magnetism 18
Miles on Horse's Foot and Horse Shoeing 37
———————— on Horse's Teeth and Stables....... 37
Mill (J.) on the Mind 10
———— (J. S.) on Liberty................... 9
———————— Subjection of Women....... 9
———————— on Representative Government 9
———————— Utilitarianism...... 9
————'s Autobiography 6
———————— Dissertations and Discussions 9
———————— Essays on Religion &c. 20
———————— Hamilton's Philosophy 9
———————— System of Logic 9
Mill's Political Economy 9
———————— Unsettled Questions 9
Miller's Elements of Chemistry 23
———————— Inorganic Chemistry............. 20

Minto's (Lord) Life and Letters............ 6
Mitchell's Manual of Architecture........... 25
———————— Manual of Assaying 28
Modern Novelist's Library 34
Monsell's 'Spiritual Songs' 31
Moore's Irish Melodies, Illustrated......... 35
———————— Lalla Rookh, Illustrated 35
Morell's Elements of Psychology 11
———————— Mental Philosophy 11
Morris's French Revolution 3
Müller's Chips from a German Workshop . 18
———————— Science of Language......... 12
———————— Science of Religion 5

New Testament Illustrated with Wood Engravings from the Old Masters......... 24
Northcott on Lathes and Turning........... 20

O'Conor's Commentary on Hebrews 30
———————— Romans 30
———————— St. John 30
Odling's Course of Practical Chemistry ... 24
Owen's Comparative Anatomy and Physiology of Vertebrate Animals 20
Owen's Lectures on the Invertebrata 20

Packe's Guide to the Pyrenees 33
Pattison's Casaubon...................... 7
Payen's Industrial Chemistry............... 26
Pewtner's Comprehensive Specifier 39
Pierce's Chess Problems 39
Pole's Game of Whist 39
Prendergast's Mastery of Languages 15
Present-Day Thoughts, by A. K. H. B. 13
Proctor's Astronomical Essays 17
———————— Moon 17
———————— Orbs around Us 17
———————— Other Worlds than Ours 17
———————— Saturn 17
———————— Scientific Essays (New Series) ... 20
———————— Sun 17
———————— Transits of Venus 17
———————— Two Star Atlases......... 16
———————— Universe 17
Public Schools Atlas 16
———————— Modern Geography 16
———————— Ancient Geography 16

Rankin on Strains in Trusses................. 28
Rawlinson's Parthia........................ 4
———————— Sassanians 4
Recreations of a Country Parson 13
Redgrave's Dictionary of Artists 24
Reilly's Map of Mont Blanc 37
———————— Monte Rosa......... 37
Reynardson's Down the Road 9
Rich's Dictionary of Antiquities 15
River's Rose Amateur's Guide 22
Rogers's Eclipse of Faith.................... 9
———————— Defence of Eclipse of Faith 9
———————— Essays.................. 9

Roget's Thesaurus of English Words and Phrases 14
Ronald's Fly-Fisher's Entomology 37
Rothschild's Israelites 30
Russell on the Christian Religion 6
———— English Constitution 2
————'s Recollections and Suggestions ... 2

Sandars's Justinian's Institutes 10
Sanford's English Kings 2
Savory's Geometric Turning 26
Schellen's Spectrum Analysis 18
Scott's Albert Durer 24
———— Papers on Civil Engineering 28
Seaside Musing, by A. K. H. B. 13
Seebohm's Oxford Reformers of 1498 3
———— Protestant Revolution 6
Sewell's History of the Early Church 5
———— Passing Thoughts on Religion.. 31
———— Preparation for Communion 31
———— Principles of Education 14
———— Readings for Confirmation 31
———— Readings for Lent 31
———— Examination for Confirmation ... 31
———— Stories and Tales 35
———— Thoughts for the Age 31
———— Thoughts for the Holy Week...... 31
Short's Post-office Gazetteer 16
Shelley's Workshop Appliances 20
Short's Church History 5
Simpson's Meeting the Sun 32
Smith's Paul's Voyage and Shipwreck...... 30
———— (*Sydney*) Essays 12
———— Life and Letters............. 7
———— Miscellaneous Works 12
———— Wit and Wisdom 12
———— (Dr. R. A.) Air and Rain 18
Snyd's Cylicut 34
Southey's Doctor 13
———— Poetical Works................. 35
Stanley's History of British Birds 21
Stephen's Ecclesiastical Biography.......... 7
———— Freethinking and Plainspeaking 9
Stepping Stones (the Series) 40
Stirling's Secret of Hegel 11
———— Sir William Hamilton 11
Stonehenge on the Dog 37
———— on the Greyhound 37
Sunday Afternoons at the Parish Church of a University City, by A. K. H. B. 13
Supernatural Religion 31

Taylor's History of India 3
———— Manual of Ancient History 6
———— Manual of Modern History 6
———— (*Jeremy*) Works, edited by *Eden* 31
Text-Books of Science...................... 19
Thirlwell's History of Greece 4

Thomson's Laws of Thought 11
Thorpe's Quantitative Analysis 20
———— and *Muir's* Qualitative Analysis ... 20
Thudichum's Chemical Physiology 23
Todd (A.) on Parliamentary Government... 2
———— and *Bowman's* Anatomy and Physiology of Man 24
Trench's Realities of Irish Life 12
Trollope's Barchester Towers.............. 39
———— Warden 39
Tyndall's American Lectures on Light ... 20
———— Belfast Address 19
———— Diamagnetism 20
———— Fragments of Science.......... 19
———— Hours of Exercise in the Alps... 33
———— Lectures on Electricity 20
———— Lectures on Light 20
———— Lectures on Sound 20
———— Heat a Mode of Motion 20
———— Molecular Physics............. 20

Ueberweg's System of Logic 11
Ure's Dictionary of Arts, Manufactures, and Mines 27

Warburton's Edward the Third 6
Watson's Geometry 20
Watts's Dictionary of Chemistry 24
Webb's Objects for Common Telescopes ... 18
Weinhold's Experimental Physics.......... 19
Wellington's Life, by *Gleig* 8
Whately's English Synonymes 14
———— Life and Correspondence........ 6
———— Logic 10
———— Rhetoric 10
White and *Donkin's* English Dictionary... 15
———— and *Riddle's* Latin Dictionaries ... 15
Whitworth on Guns and Steel 27
Wilcocks's Sea-Fisherman 36
Williams's Aristotle's Ethics.............. 10
Willis's Principles of Mechanism.......... 26
Willoughby's (Lady) Diary................. 34
Wood's Bible Animals 22
———— Homes without Hands 21
———— Insects at Home............... 21
———— Insects Abroad 21
———— Out of Doors 21
———— Strange Dwellings 21

Yonge's English-Greek Lexicons 16
———— Horace 36
Youatt on the Dog 37
———— on the Horse 36

Zeller's Socrates 5
———— Stoics, Epicureans, and Sceptics... 5

www.ingramcontent.com/pod-product-compliance
Lightning Source LLC
Chambersburg PA
CBHW030835270326
41928CB00007B/1068